INTRODUCTIO
GRAPHIC DES

A GUIDE TO THINKING, PROCESS & STYLE

DATE

Bloomsbury Visual Arts
An imprint of Bloomsbury Publishing Plc

50 Bedford Square	1385 Broadway
London	New York
WC1B 3DP	NY 10018
UK	USA

www.bloomsbury.com

BLOOMSBURY and the Diana logo are trademarks of Bloomsbury Publishing Plc

British Library Cataloguing-in-Publication Data
A catalogue record for this book is available from the British Library.

ISBN:
PB: 978-1-4725-8929-3
ePDF: 978-1-4725-8930-9

Library of Congress Cataloging-in-Publication Data
Names: Sherin, Aaris, author.
Title: Introduction to graphic design : a guide to thinking, process and style / Aaris Sherin.
Description: New York : Bloomsbury Visual Arts, 2018.
Identifiers: LCCN 2016049178 | ISBN 9781472589293 (paperback)
Subjects: LCSH: Graphic arts. | Commercial art. | BISAC: DESIGN / Graphic Arts / General.
Classification: LCC NC997 .S457 2018 | DDC 741.6--dc23 LC record available at https://lccn.loc.gov/2016049178

Series: Required Reading Range

Cover design: Louise Dugdale

Typeset by Struktur Design
Printed and bound in China

To find out more about our authors and books visit www.bloomsbury.com. Here you will find extracts, author interviews, details of forthcoming events and the option to sign up for our newsletters.

INTRODUCTION TO GRAPHIC DESIGN:

A GUIDE TO THINKING, PROCESS & STYLE

AARIS SHERIN

Bloomsbury Visual Arts
An imprint of Bloomsbury Publishing Plc

B L O O M S B U R Y
LONDON · OXFORD · NEW YORK · NEW DELHI · SYDNEY

PREFACE

This text focuses on the formal structures of graphic design and how visual concepts can be applied to print and screen-based applications as well as three-dimensional outputs such as packaging and signage. By focusing on critical thinking, the application of visual exploration, and the special relationships associated with placement and layout, we will be taking a systematic approach to the process of creative problem solving.

The goal of *Introduction to Graphic Design* is to demystify the fundamental concepts and critical thinking skills needed to successfully complete design projects. In essence, this book acts as a shortcut or extended visual notes. Relevant terminology is included as are basic rules of typography and layout. With concise and straightforward information, this book provides answers to common questions and information about how to achieve successful results using systems of arrangement and basic visual elements. There are always challenges in graphic design, so looking at ways to understand these challenges and to overcome them is part of what we will explore. Many of the topics included in this text are covered in greater depth in other books, and readers are encouraged to build on what they learn with further investigation. Basically, this book aims to give first-year design students the confidence to balance the mixture of structure and experimentation needed to effectively give visual form to concepts and ideas.

HOW TO USE THIS BOOK: FOR STUDENTS

For many of you, this text will be your first introduction to the principles of graphic design. There is a lot to learn, and the terminology and concepts of graphic design can seem overwhelming. Pay special attention to the *Key Terms and Concepts* sections at the beginning of each chapter. They will quickly familiarize you with the language of design. Then, as you read though the text content, keep an eye out for those same terms and scrutinize how they are used in the narrative.

At the end of each chapter there is a list of the *Chapter in Review: Do's and Don'ts*. These sections reinforce what you should have learned while reading the text in each chapter. As you work on class assignments, you can refer back to the *Do's and Don'ts*. Keep in mind that design principles provide guidelines rather than a set of absolute rules. How specific *Do's and Don'ts* apply to your assignments will vary depending on the goals of the project and specific directions from your instructor. If you aren't sure how a particular rule or principle applies to your project, look at the image examples in the text and see if they relate to what you are working on and ask an instructor for help.

VISUAL LEARNERS

Most artists and designers are primarily visual learners. The diagrams and visual examples of professional design work directly relate to the text content. Sometimes seeing is easier than reading, and you may need to study the visual examples to fully understand how the text content relates to real-life design projects. As you go through the text and look at the images, imagine how you might apply the concepts highlighted to your school assignments. Discuss the ideas presented in the text with classmates and examine which of the image examples you like best. Assess these designs critically. Are you drawn to work with a particular style? Does color make you notice some pieces more than others? Do the projects presented target a particular type of consumer or audience? And, finally, what would you have done differently if you were asked to redesign the professional projects in the book?

LINEAR STRUCTURE

Most books are linear. They begin with a table of contents and sequentially move through a series of chapters. Because a book is bound or stitched together along the spine, chapters cannot be physically reorganized or reordered by the reader. This fixed placement means that the assignments you work on in class may not follow the linear structure set up by this text. That's okay. Not every semester is the same length, students at different schools take courses at different times, and instructors have their own preference for how to teach graphic design. While the text content of this book is fixed, how you use it shouldn't be. Your instructor will assign sections of the text so they relate to the projects you are working on at specific points in the semester. Some readers may read Chapter 6 before Chapter 3, whereas others will completely skip the sections in Chapter 8 on finishing and binding because their programs focus on digital rather than print-based media.

Being a graphic design student is hard work, but it is also a lot of fun. As you go through this text and work on class assignments, don't forget to take time to enjoy the pleasure of seeing a well-executed project or the intricate forms of a new typeface. The more time you spend looking at visual work and practicing your design skills the easier it will be to produce successful projects.

HOW TO USE THIS BOOK: FOR EDUCATORS

As a long-time teacher and part-time administrator, I, along with my colleagues, constantly come up against the formidable challenges of planning what should be taught in introductory graphic design classes. Students come from a wide range of backgrounds, and what is required varies considerably depending on the size of the program, the overall curricula, and the faculty doing the teaching. Sometimes introductory design classes focus almost exclusively on software skills, whereas other schools teach software in dedicated technology courses and students work on studio projects with little or no software training by the instructor.

At my own institution we teach a combination of design principles and technical skills in a class that is simply titled *Introduction to Graphic Design*. Visual projects and short exercises provide opportunities to use design principles and experiment with layout and arrangement, while students learn technology via demonstrations and exercises. In talking to fellow educators at my own and at other institutions, this model is popular for both pedagogical and practical reasons. Many design programs are chronically understaffed, and the reality of running a separate class to teach software can be burdensome. More importantly, design educators see lasting value in pairing technical and conceptual/visual skills right from the beginning of a student's education.

Anyone who has sat in on multiple sections of the same class knows that there is no single way to successfully teach design. Individual styles vary, and what works well for one instructor will be different from what works for another. This text is designed to be flexible and to accommodate diverse teaching styles and the differences in curricula. It focuses on principles and visual exercises while acknowledging the importance of software and technical skills in design education. Specific tutorials are widely available for free online and through subscription-based services like Lynda.com. To avoid the risk of being immediately dated and overly specific, the text avoids wading into this already over-crowded arena.

Educators are encouraged to see chapters as individual modules where ideas are gathered around one or more themes but are not overly prescriptive. Chapters can be assigned in the order they appear in the table of contents, or students can dip in and out of the text in a sequence that more closely follows the ordering of projects in a particular instructor's class. The *Chapter in Review: Do's and Don'ts* emphasize principles discussed in the chapter and provide review points for students while the *Key Terms and Concepts* at the beginning of each chapter introduce readers to important design terminology before they are confronted with the words used in context. My hope is for this text to provide useful information and concepts that will allow both educators and students to explore some of the most fundamental principles of graphic design.

CHAPTER 1:
Overview of the Field

KEY TERMS AND CONCEPTS:

Advertising design is a subsection of design focused particularly on creating visuals, experiences, and environments used for the purposes of promotion. (p. 14)

Assets are items such as text, imagery, textures, and other visual elements that will be used in a design project. Assets may be given to you as part of an assignment, or you may have to find or create your own assets. (p. 20)

Audience refers to specific people the design is targeted toward. Designers often spend time defining their audience so they can effectively target to those people's preferences. (p. 10)

Client is the person or company that hires a designer. (p. 10)

Commercial artist is a term that predates the term graphic design. (p. 14)

Communication Design (see *graphic design*) (p. 10)

Concept is the idea behind a design. (pp. 16, 18)

Contract work refers to non-permanent employment. Like freelance, it can either be part or full time, and contract employees can be paid by the hour or by the job. (p. 25)

Design thinking is a term used to describe a range of cognitive-based processes used in problem solving. The term was popularized by Tim Brown in his 2009 book *Change by Design*. (p. 18)

First Things First is a manifesto that was initially written in the 1960s by Ken Garland. Visual communicators who signed the document challenged fellow designers to turn away from purely commercial interests and put their skills to "worthwhile use." (p. 14)

Freelancing/freelancers are independent designers who take on individual projects and work either in a home studio or at a client's office. Independent freelancers may be paid by the hour or can quote a set price for an entire job. (p. 25)

Graphic artist is a historical term used to refer to layout professionals before the term *graphic design* was used. (p. 14)

Graphic design is the process or practice of combining visual material, usually text, imagery, and other elements, to communicate a message or to create an experience for an audience. The terms *communication design* and *visual communication design* are used interchangeably with the term graphic design. (p. 10)

Interface design is a creative process used to produce interactive, digitally based experiences, environments, and services. (p. 12)

Industrial design (also called *product design*) is a process that uses creative ideas, critical thinking, and testing to create mass-produced objects and systems. (p. 14)

Interactive design (also called *Interaction Design* and *IxD*) is the process of designing products, experiences and services which a person will interact with. Often people associate interactive design with work that will be seen or used with a screen but interactive designers can produce products and objects as well. (p. 12)

Motion graphics uses a combination of video footage, still images, type, and audio to create multimedia designs. (p. 15)

Print production refers to physically printing designs on a digital or offset printer. (p. 15)

Screen-based design refers to design work that is intended to be seen and/or used on a screen. (p. 15)

Visual communication or visual communication design (see *graphic design*) (p. 10)

Web design is design, layout, and interaction that will be seen and/or used on the internet. (p. 15)

WHAT IS GRAPHIC DESIGN?

Graphic design is the process or practice of combining visual material, usually text, imagery, and other elements, to communicate a message or to create an experience for an audience. Successful design occurs when a message or experience is optimally expressed.

IS GRAPHIC DESIGN ART?

Designers use many of the same media, tools, and techniques as artists, but the goals of fine art and design are different. Unlike fine art, where the creator is expressing a personal vision, the designer produces visual material within a more controlled setting. In design, a client's message has to be expressed to a given audience. For print, packaging, or environmental design, cost and production considerations make up a large part of the designer's responsibility, and—regardless of the media used—the designer must consider how the physical context of where the design will be seen affects its success. What separates design from art is intent and purpose. Rather than finding structure limiting, the designer makes the most of constraints. This doesn't mean designers don't produce art or artists don't design. There is a fuzzy area between the two disciplines, and practitioners in both fields create innovative work that blurs the lines between the two. For the purposes of this text, graphic design (also known as communication or visual communication design) is defined as a professional client-based activity where practitioners focus on expressing a message to an audience, delivering content to an end user, or engaging an end user in a particular set of activities.

above and right

Not all design work is client based. Self-promotions offer designers the opportunity to let loose and have some fun.

Design: This is Folly, Minneapolis, Minnesota

above

Communication designers create experiences as well as objects and printed material. The design for the museum exhibit includes a space where visitors can participate in the exhibition by drawings on the walls.

Design: Marko Rašić & Vedrana Vrabec, Zagreb, Croatia

right

Barbara Kruger worked in advertising before she started making artwork. Now she is primarily known as an artist but she still uses the visual language of design as seen in these details of her Belief + Doubt installation at the Hirshhorn Museum in Washington, DC. Her work is a good example of artwork blurring the boundaries between art and design.

WHAT DOES A DESIGNER PRODUCE?

In the past, graphic design was primarily concerned with two-dimensional spaces like books, magazines, posters, and fliers. Today the range of outputs produced by designers can include three-dimensional objects and digital/virtual space. Designers are regularly tasked with giving form to content that is intended to be viewed on devices including computers, tablets, smartphones, and other consoles. They also produce three-dimensional outputs like packaging, signage, installations, and displays. While the physical form expressed by design takes has broadened, the underlying principles for arrangement, structure, and expression have not changed.

Different media may require a range of diverse skill sets. For instance, an interactive designer is expected to understand principles of user interface design whereas a position in an interactive design studio might require employees to understand the nuances of paper choice and print production. All designers need to understand the formal principles of design, work well with typography, and have excellent visual and spatial skills. Regardless of what type of design you intend to focus on, it is important to begin by learning the basic principles of form making, typography, and concept development. A strong foundation in these skills is transferable to all areas of graphic design.

GRAPHIC DESIGNERS PRODUCE:

Blogs

Social media content

Brochures

Virtual reality platforms

Packaging

Magazines

Posters

Marketing materials

Mobile apps

Interactive kiosks

Screens for websites

Books

Identities/logos

Direct mail

Promotions materials

User interfaces

Game design

Advertising

Motion graphics

Kiosk interfaces

Signage

Retail design

Broadcast design

Branding materials

left

The design of the interior for this frozen yogurt bar called *Chill* provided an opportunity to create a visually integrated space and is an example of communication designers working in three-dimensional space.

Design: Kuhlmann Leavitt, St. Louis, Missouri

right

Adding custom visuals like drawings or illustration can make products more appealing to consumers and allows a designer to use his/her drawing or illustration skills.

Design Eduardo Bertone, Madrid, Spain

left

Application design is an important subsection of interactive design. When designing applications, the designer has to focus on function and creating an optimal user experience as well as the visual appearance.

Design: B12, Scottsdale, Arizona

THE DUAL RESPONSIBILITY OF THE DESIGNER

Graphic designers act as intermediaries between the client and the end user or audience, and as such designers have responsibility to both groups. In the beginning and mid-twentieth century, industrialization gave rise to the development of new goods and services, and design was used to provide visual form and the persuasive muscle needed to encourage people to make purchases. Early industrial designers and "graphic or commercial artists" (the terms predating graphic design) worked to create visuals and products for clients. Advertisers tapped into unmet aspirations and exploited consumers' subconscious motivations, but the real needs of users and audiences were largely absent from measures of success.

The notion of what constituted successful design was questioned as early as 1964, when twenty-two visual communicators signed a manifesto called *First Things First* that challenged designers to put their skills to "worthwhile use." Then in the 1970s, industrial designer Victor Papanek wrote *Design for the Real World*, in which he argued that designers had an obligation to work for the greater good and not just the financial well-being of their clients. In his follow-up book, *The Green Imperative*, Papanek focused primarily on environmental issues and he questioned "whether designers, architects, and engineers can be held personally responsible and legally liable for creating tools, objects, appliances, and buildings that bring about environmental deterioration." At the time, colleagues and even his professional organization denounced Papanek's ideas, but today both industrial and graphic designers have largely accepted the underlying principles of greater responsibility put forth by Papanek and the signatories of *First Things First*.

above

Sustainable design often focuses on specifying eco-friendly paper, printing, and other materials, but it can also involve working for like-minded organizations and providing them with great design so they can be economically viable.

Design: This is Folly, Minneapolis, Minnesota

right

The book *Ground|Water* challenges traditional methods of conveying scientific information to the public. The designers' goal was to create a sustainably produced object that showcased the intense visual nature of the book's content, which includes fine art, design, and architecture.

Design: Cast Iron Design, Boulder, Colorado

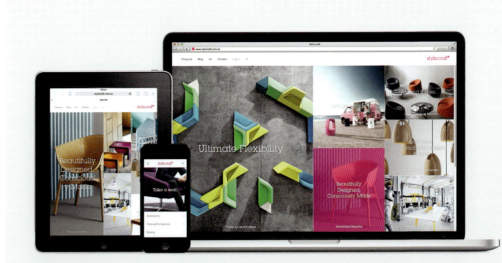

PRINT VERSUS SCREEN-BASED DESIGN

As we have discussed, there are numerous areas of specialization in graphic design. One of the most common ways to categorize design is based on whether the end result will be seen on screen or in print. Screen-based design has many subspecialties, including web design, user interface/experience design, motion graphics, and interactive design. In print design, the audience sees a physical output. These diverse deliverables include books, billboards, wedding invitations, restaurant menus, and posters. Not all design projects fit neatly into these two categories. Packaging and environmental signage exist as physical objects, but they are not always printed, and branding and visual identities exist both on screen and in print. Similarly, design for social media exists entirely on screen but may be still or use motion depending on where the final application will be seen.

The fundamental principles for working with and arranging visual elements are applicable to both screen-based and print design. Many of the differences between these types of design are centered on techniques and competencies used in production. The explanation of production practices detailed in Chapter 8 primarily focuses on how to present simple print-based projects. Most graphic design programs offer classes that specifically teach fundamental competencies for digital production and interactivity. Since understanding how to effectively design for digital and print outputs is equally important, content callouts within subsequent chapters will highlight layout and arrangement considerations that apply particularly to screen-based designs.

WHY *RULES* ARE IMPORTANT

There are numerous examples of well-known designers who produce successful communications pieces while seeming to break fundamental rules of design. That being said, the aim of most visual communication is to help users/viewers navigate through visual material. In order to achieve this deceptively simple goal, the designer needs to meet the objectives set out in a project brief or assignment, and content needs to be clearly communicated. Rules are simply a tool to help designers successfully give form to concepts. The Chapter in Review Do's and Don'ts sections include essential strategies for working with visual elements and text. While experienced designers may choose to break the rules or the guidelines outlined in the following chapters, you need to know the rules first in order to know when and how it is appropriate to break them. Ultimately, design is both utilitarian and experimental, and the designer reserves the right to decide when to maintain and when to break free of structure.

INSPIRATION

Inspiration is a key element of the creative process, and while some designers may seem to pull ideas out of thin air, in most cases ongoing observation and analysis are a constant part of a designer's life. Looking at other people's work is one of the best ways to develop an understanding of how visuals and text can be combined to produce effective design. The more you explore and look at examples of design, the easier it will be to recognize what works and what doesn't work, thus further developing your analytical skills. Seeing how others have approached similar problems can be particularly important as you start out in the field since this type of analysis provides a foundation for advanced research practices. When you see something you like, you may be tempted to imitate someone else's style. Copying is inappropriate both in school and in professional situations. Use inspiration to learn about how design problems are solved but always try to produce your own original solutions for projects. While design annuals and magazines can be a useful source for finding and identifying engaging visual work, it is now easier to find visual material online.

above and right

The designers used basic design principles including repetition and consistent use of negative space (see p. 70) to help these collateral materials visually relate to each other and to the exterior design of delivery trucks.

Design Izyum Creative Group, Kiev, Ukraine

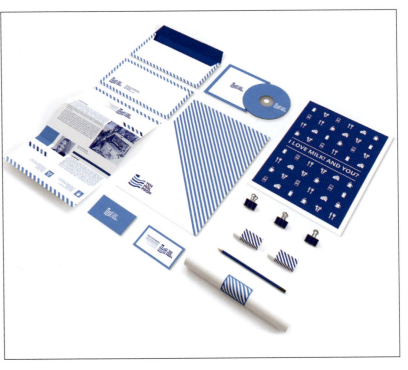

above

Sometime creating engaging visual design is more important than following the rules. Here, the designers for the offices of Credit Suisse in Singapore used whimsical graphics to create an interior space with visuals not normally associated with a financial institution.

Design: THERE, Surry Hill, Australia

above

Design: Acme, Paris, France

left

It is important to look at all sorts of inspiration before embarking on a design. The identity and packaging for this organic juice company uses croppings of paint splatter as texture rather than a photo or illustration of actual juice.

Design: Izyum Creative Group, Kiev, Ukraine

Online content and image sharing sites make it easy to access and catalog design content. This exercise focuses on how to identify and evaluate creative work using blogs, websites, and mobile apps.

Begin by creating an account with pinterest.com, tumblr.com, or another content sharing site (these sites are free and easy to use). Then create albums, boards, or folders with specific themes (see image example on p. 18). For instance, you might have one or two albums/boards of work related to class projects and a couple of others to keep track of design examples that interest you personally. By using search engines and visiting websites of companies you are familiar with, you should be able to begin to identify design work where the use of formal elements or concepts is similar to the projects you are working on. Add these examples to your account or boards.

After you have found several examples, make notes about how each piece relates to your current assignments. Show your boards or folders to an instructor to ensure the "inspiration" you are looking at adequately matches the goals of the class projects. Try to avoid looking exclusively at design work with the same content or theme as the projects you are working on. Instead, look for similar outputs or end products (e.g., page layouts or posters) that highlight innovative ways of using type, image, and compositional space to communicate information. Content sharing sites make it easy to see what your friends and classmates are looking at by following either their accounts or particular albums or boards. This is a great way to see what appeals to and resonates with other designers.

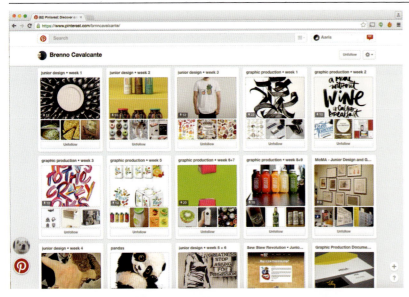

TECHNICAL SKILLS

Technology is ubiquitous in the contemporary experience. Where a home personal computer and television were once the extent of most people's experience with media, today we have Fitbits, smart watches, and a plethora of other devices and applications designed to mediate and enhance our experience of the world around us. Since we eat, sleep, and work with devices at our side, it's easy to think that mastering applications and software is the key to creating successful graphic design. In fact the opposite is true. Yes, a graphic designer needs to know how to use Adobe Photoshop, Illustrator, and InDesign (among others). That's a given, but understanding how to use these programs does not make one a graphic designer. This distinction is important for several reasons. The software programs needed to produce graphic design are constantly in flux. During the years a typical undergraduate student spends in school, he/she is likely to see a number of significant changes to software platforms and sometimes to production processes as well. Secondly, graphic designers are primarily visual communicators and the mediators of messages and/or user experiences. These design proficiencies, sometimes referred to as design thinking or design concept skills, are infinitely more important than software. In short, learning software is relatively easy; developing concepts or ideas and learning to work with type, color, texture, and image is harder and more nuanced, but it is also more rewarding. Students who struggle to learn software are usually able to catch up, whereas students who struggle to create effective visual material and develop concepts and have trouble with working with typography remain at a disadvantage well into their professional careers.

above

Pinterest lets you save images and examples of projects and other inspiration on separate boards. This is a great way to keep track of designs and other visual material.

right

Sometimes inspiration comes from unexpected places. South African designer Garth Walker draws inspiration from the world around him and uses personal photography to document visuals he finds inspiring.

Design: Garth Walker, Durban, South Africa

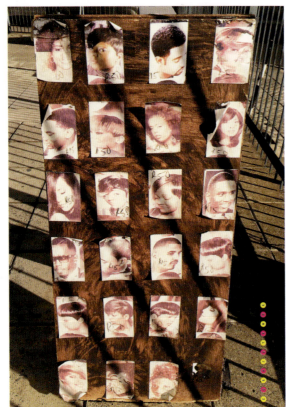

left

Graphic designers need a combination of technical and conceptual skills. They often also need to be able to produce things by hand. For this holiday gift, designers at Dedica had the task of creating and producing unique packaging by hand.

Design: Dedica Group, New York

SOFTWARE TUTORIALS

Numerous companies provide online resources for learning software skills. Free sites include one-off tutorials and forums where users ask questions and receive answers from other users or "experts." Fee-based subscription services such as Lynda.com offer some of the best video-based software instruction on the market. Lynda.com has lower-priced student subscription rates, and some colleges and universities have an institutional package allowing all students to access tutorials at no additional cost. For free tutorials check out Adobe.com or Youtube.com or type exactly what you want to learn into a search engine like Google and check out various video- and forum-based options.

right

Designers printed, sprayed glass, and generally experimented with different lettering, materials, and printing/cutting techniques.

Design: Dedica Group, New York

WHO DESIGNERS WORK WITH

Once you begin working as designer you will need to learn how to collaborate with other professionals who will help you gather the assets or raw material needed for a project and others who will help you produce the final product.

Interactive designers work with teams of developers and programmers who create the back-end coding required for interactive projects to function correctly, and they assist teams whose job it is to test a product, site, or other interface before bringing it to market or a live launch. If you work for a large company there may be a strategist who helps ensure the goals of a project match the preferences of the intended audience, and many companies also employ project managers and support staff to help make sure jobs are finished on time and are produced within the allotted budget. Print and packaging designers use the services of a professional printer or manufacturer to produce final printed and three-dimensional objects. And designers working in many areas collaborate with marketers to develop an overall project plan or strategy. In school it is often difficult to mimic the collaborative environment designers find in their first jobs, but working in small groups and teaming up with students from other majors is a great way to get a taste of what it is like to work on real-world projects.

Since there are so many subspecialties in graphic design, it is impossible to list all the related fields a designer may work with in a professional setting. Below are of some of the most common types of professionals a graphic designer collaborates with when producing work for clients.

Programmers

Developers

Software engineers

Writers/editors

Content producers

Video editors and producers

Sales professionals

Media buyers/specialists

Strategists

Marketers

Project managers

Photographers

Illustrators

Animators

Production designers

Printers

Fabricators

Technologist

Ethnographer

WHO SHOULD BE A GRAPHIC DESIGNER?

Graphic design is a teachable skill, but not everyone can be successful as a designer. Some people excel in visual pursuits while others will be better in service-based fields or working with coding rather than images and type. If you are not sure whether you are well suited for a career in graphic design, consider the following questions. If you answer "no" to several points below, you might want to speak with an advisor or instructor and discuss whether a career in graphic design is right for you.

- Do you enjoy art and design-making projects (either ones you completed in school or in your spare time)?

- Do you enjoy the challenge of solving problems and developing new ideas? Sometimes designers work without a narrow brief and look for problems to solve. Possessing a heightened sense of curiosity is helpful.

- Are you comfortable working within structured parameters and with defined goals?

- Do you enjoy coming up with new ideas and experimenting with formal elements such as shape, line, color, and type?

- Are you happy working at a computer for hours on end? While good graphic design isn't necessarily dependent on software, realistically most designers spend a large portion of their days in front of a computer.

- Are you comfortable working in a constantly evolving field? While it is generally true that formal and critical thinking skills are the most important competencies one learns in college, design software does continue to be updated and designers are required to keep up with the programs.

- Do you enjoy looking at design and do you find it stimulating to produce class projects? This doesn't necessarily mean that you have to be successful at every project or be pleased with the result, but it really helps to be interested in what you are doing.

- Are you comfortable revising work based on feedback from teachers and fellow classmates?

Some students come into art or design programs knowing exactly what they want to do when they graduate, but more often college is a time of discovery and experimentation. It is not unusual to identify your chosen area of design expertise only in the final year of school. And sometimes you may need to spend time in a professional setting before deciding that a particular media suits you best. Even after graduation it is not uncommon for designers at the beginning of their careers to try several work situations before finally choosing a path closely matched to their interests and skill sets.

above

Rick Griffith, director of Matter, a graphic design studio and print shop, in his office in Denver, Colorado. Some designers work in corporate offices but others are employed as freelancers or in creative studios where turntables, bean bag chairs, and table tennis are among the perks employees enjoy.

CAREER OUTLOOK

Given the financial challenges entailed by years of study, it is reasonable to want assurance that if you attain a degree in graphic design, you will have a good chance of starting your career. While there are no guarantees, the good news is that graphic design is an employable skill, and most students who do well and apply themselves to the job search will have the skills needed to find entry-level employment.

Creative firms exist all over the world, but graphic design and its related fields do tend to be somewhat location dependent. There are higher concentrations of companies using creative professionals in urban areas and, therefore, more jobs in these locations. Graphic design graduates who come from rural settings often move to cities to seek employment, but if one is motivated and good at self-promotion it is still possible to be a designer outside of big cities. The Internet, Skype, and file sharing programs enable people to make connections, to collaborate, and to find clients regardless of their geographic location. In specialties like motion graphics and interaction design, it is common for animators, illustrators, and designers to work together on a project without ever meeting in person. Online job sites, including those hosted by professional design organizations, make it possible to look for and apply for jobs in a variety of locations. Many of these sites also offer opportunities to post online portfolios and network with professionals working in a particular specialization or area of design.

above

Lotta Nieminen works in a variety of areas related to design including illustration, art direction, and styling for photo shoots.

Design: Lotta Nieminen, New York

right

Hand drawn type and catchy phrases make this office space feel unique and inviting. Client work makes up most of the jobs done by graphic designers, but there are opportunities to do more whimsical personal work as well.

Design: THERE, Surry Hill, Australia

INTERNSHIPS

Internships are an excellent way of getting on-the-job experience while trying out different types of design employment. Many undergraduate design programs include an internship option or work requirement as part of the curriculum, and in some cases students are even placed directly in work situations by their program or school. Regardless of whether an internship is compulsory, it is a good idea to consider doing at least one or two internships before graduation. Leaving school with work experience makes finding a first full-time position easier, and some students are even hired directly from internships. As long as the company or organization clearly states what your responsibilities will be ahead of time, internships tend to be worthwhile regardless of whether they offer monetary compensation.

above

The owner of this Paris graphic design studio helps her interns as they solve design problems. Interning is a great way to put the skills you learn in school to use in a real-world setting.

left

People work in all types of spaces but are often happiest when the space reflects their own interests. Here concept is key, and the visuals applied to these elevators provide a bit of levity to the office environment.

Design: THERE, Surry Hill, Australia

TYPICAL JOB CATEGORIES AND TITLES FOR DESIGNERS

Owner/founder

The owners, founders, and partners of creative companies use a variety of titles depending on the size and structure of their organization. These positions may involve hands-on design or they may be focused on strategy, client relations, and management.

- CEO
- Partner
- Principle

Managerial

Managerial positions will focus on overseeing other designers and possibly design support staff. Depending on the position, they may involve hands-on design work or they may primarily be focused on strategy and project management.

- Creative director
- Design manager
- Vice president (for instance VP of user experience design)
- Chief creative officer
- Brand manager/strategist

Creative/upper-level design

These positions are primarily hands-on design jobs. They also usually involve working directly with clients and/or management. Titles will vary depending on the responsibilities entailed by the position and the scope of the organization.

- Art director
- Designer
- Senior designer
- Associate art director
- Media producer
- Web designer
- Interaction designer
- Multimedia designer
- Graphic designer
- Creative consultant
- Lead designer
- Digital designer
- Content/digital strategist
- Visual designer
- User interface/experience (UI, UX) designer
- Social media manager

Entry level

These jobs are entry-level positions, which involve working directly with upper-level designers and professionals in other areas of a company. They often involve both production and design responsibilities.

- Assistant art director
- Junior (graphic) designer
- Assistant designer
- Communications assistant
- Designer/animator
- Graphic artist
- Digital content creator/producer/developer
- Social media content designer

Support level

Jobs in this category encompass both entry-level and volunteer positions, and they usually focus on providing technical and production support to a team or group of designers.

- Graphic design assistant
- Support specialist
- Production designer
- Intern

FREELANCE AND CONTRACT WORK

Freelancers are independent designers who take on individual projects and work either in a home studio or at a client's office. Independent freelancers may be paid by the hour, or they can quote a set price for an entire job. Talent agencies also place freelancers in companies where short-term design help is needed; in these situations a designer usually works in-house and is paid by the agency as opposed to directly by the client. Motion graphics, animation, and interaction design are all areas of design specialization where freelancing is common.

A contract position refers to a job where a designer works a set number of full- or part-time hours but is not considered a permanent employee. Because the number of employees in contract positions is easy to scale up and down, these positions are have become more popular in small design studios and large companies alike. A contract employee may work full time, but he/she still won't have all the rights of a regular salaried employee and is often paid by a third party agency rather than by the organization itself. Large companies often hire entry-level designers in contract positions, and while these jobs are often considered less secure and therefore less desirable than permanent positions, they can pay just as much as a full-time salaried position and can be a good option for recent graduates.

above

Many designers work in companies or at design studios and advertising agencies, but some choose to work for as freelancers. Freelancers may specialize in a specific type of job or client, but designers like Esen Karol, who has a one-person studio in Istanbul, take on work form both arts organizations and corporate clients.

Design: Esen Karol, Istanbul, Turkey

right

Brazilian designer Felipe Taborda has a small studio where he employs one or two assistants. Unlike Esen Karol he primarily works for arts and culture organizations.

Design: Felipe Taborda, Rio de Janeiro, Brazil

CHAPTER 2: Concepts and Ideas

KEY TERMS AND CONCEPTS:

Brief is a written document outlining the specific expectations of a design project. The brief is usually developed by the client but may also be initiated by a design company or designer. (p. 28)

Brainstorming uses lists, diagrams, and sketches as an activity to help develop creative solutions. (p. 36)

Cliché is an idea, visual, or thought that is overused to the point that it lacks originality and loses the ability to carry original meaning. (p. 35)

Context is the physical or digital space where a design will exist. (pp. 28, 32)

Craft is similar to neatness and refers to how well a two- or three-dimensional item or printout is displayed (including on screen) or constructed. (p. 47)

Critique is a written or verbal evaluation of a design project. The critique usually includes recommendations for what should be changed to improve the design. (p. 49)

Design process is a repeatable series of actions used to develop design projects. The design process begins with the brief and ends with *production* and dissemination of the final product to the viewer or user. (p. 28)

Ideation is the process of generating ideas and expressing them through either diagrams or visual explorations. (p. 46)

Inspiration occurs when visual or mental stimulation leads to a new idea or solution. Many design concepts begin with inspiration. (p. 35)

Production can be either digital or physical and may involve printing or coding, depending on what type of design is being made. (p. 28; for more on print production, see Chapter 8)

Research is the systematic gathering and investigation of facts, ideas, or visuals related to a particular subject or project. (p. 32)

Revision refers to redoing or changing a design, usually after receiving feedback on an initial version of a project. (p. 46)

Strategy is a plan of action designed to achieve specific goals and objectives. (p. 28)

Visual explorations refer to different ways of using visual material to communicate a message. For example, a designer will often create a number of versions or visual explorations when developing a layout. (p. 28)

DESIGN IS A CREATIVE PROCESS

Every piece of communication design is the result of the creative process. In the most basic sense, design is produced when you engage in a series of repeatable steps that are used to solve conceptually and practically based problems. Professional designers and design companies often create customized processes for use on client projects, but the basic steps in the design process remain consistent even if the language used to describe them changes. The design process can be used as a whole, or individual components can be pulled apart and used on their own. The amount of time spent on each phase of the design process varies depending on the size/scope of a project and the deadline to complete the assignment.

BEGINNING A PROJECT

A design project begins with the brief or assignment. Typically a brief tells the designer what needs to be accomplished, what kind of people the design outputs should target, how much time the designer has to work on a project, and specifics about the budget. School assignments often mimic aspects of a professional brief. They rarely contain a budget, but they may provide information about production requirements and even specific image or text assets for use in the design. After reviewing the brief or the assignment, the designer will need to conduct research (see p. 32) to find out about the client, the target audience, and the context where the final output will exist. A communications strategy or project plan is then developed. The designer then engages in brainstorming and concept development followed by ideation and visual explorations. Sketching and laying out a design using computer software are part of ideation and visual exploration. The final step for student projects is for a design to be produced digitally or physically and then presented for critique and grading. This chapter examines individual aspects of the design process and explores common techniques for engaging in brainstorming and visual design development. Subsequent chapters highlight specific formal design competencies such as color, type, and layout. As you read Chapters 3 through 8 and work on the exercises in the text or on assignments from your instructor, it may be helpful to return to this chapter and review the methods for concept development and idea generation outlined in pp. 33–41.

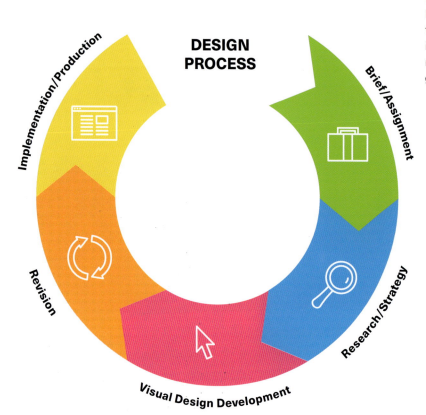

DESIGN PROCESS

Implementation/Production

Brief/Assignment

Research/Strategy

Visual Design Development

Revision

Designs are successful only if they are effective in the space or context where the audience will see them. These posters use contrast and type to stand out against the architecture around them.

Design: Project Projects, New York

This is Folly developed the name for the line of furniture and branded it to appeal to the company's target audience. The ideas for the design were inspired by the aesthetic of the "Kluk" furniture collection by Organic Design Operatives (ODO).

Design: This is Folly, Minneapolis, Minnesota

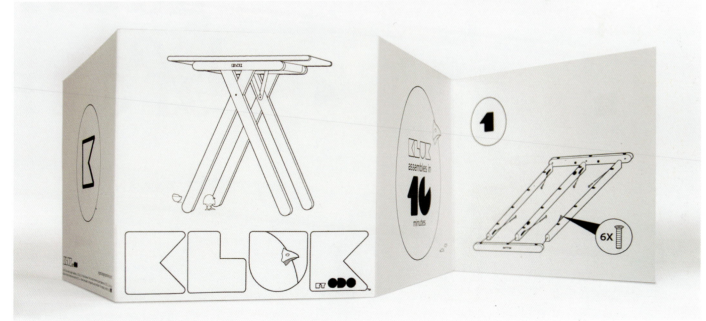

left

This example shows the process behind creating a new digital typeface. The concept for the typeface Bequeth was inspired by engravings on tombstones done in the mid-1700s. After doing research about the type of the lettering and stone carving done at the time and after looking at hundreds of gravestones, the designer chose a single stone to work from.

below

She then took rubbings of the letterforms to get as much information as possible about each letter's particular features and characteristics.

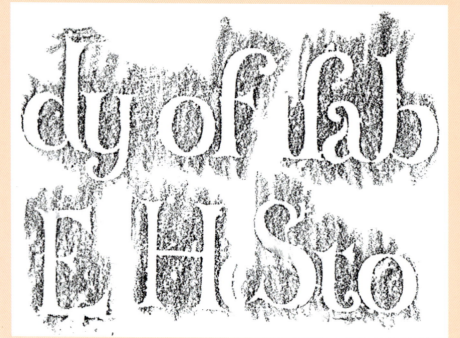

above

Because the letterforms were originally carved by hand, there were a lot of variations in the characters. Redrawing the letters in pencil helped the designer make decisions about which characteristics of each letter would work well in the digital typeface. Then the designer inked the letters to get a sense of their weight and size.

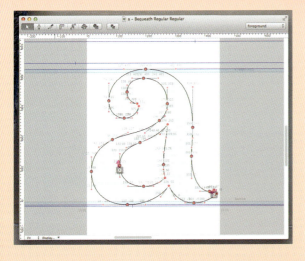

above

The next part of the design process was completed on the computer and was started only after the designer was happy with the hand-drawn letters. The designer redrew the alphabet using the program RoboFont. Here you see the detail of the letter form as the designer worked on the lowercase "a."

The Bequeath type specimen sheet:

1765 — 2014

Bequeath

in — *to*

Here Lyeth
Closed her eyes
upon a vain world

Aged 78 years
6 months and 5 days

Here underneath
resigned her breath
Interr'd the Corps

**Twice connected
with the army**
of the revolution

Beneath this

All you that stand
and view this stone
prepare for death
as I have done

**Summons Come
Saints Obey
Anno Domini**

gone to a fairer land
of pleasure & love

Sleep on thou lovely babes
And take thy peaceful Rest
The Lord has called you hence
Because he thought it Best
to join the bright band
of angels above

A soul so calm it knew no ebbs or flows
Which passion could not decompose
A female softness with a manly mind
In sickness patient & in death resigned

planted on earth
to bloom in heaven

Beloved

ABCDEFGHI
JKLMNOPQR
STUVWXYZ
abcdefghijklmn
opqrstuvwxyz
1234567890

Bequeath Regular 24 pt

**ABCDEFGHI
JKLMNOPQR
STUVWXYZ
abcdefghijklmn
opqrstuvwxyz**

Bequeath Bold 24 pt

*ABCDEFGHI
JKLMNOPQR
STUVWXYZ
abcdefghijklmn
opqrstuvwxyz*

Bequeath Italic 24 pt

Bequeath Typeface • Designed by Liz DeLuna • Type@Cooper Extended Program 2013–2014 • www.main5design.com
• with gratitude to all of my professors and classmates •

left

Special software helped the designer create additional weights or versions of the typeface, but she still had to revise the individual letters based on feedback and on self-assessment.

above

After the designer finished the typeface, she created a letterpress specimen sheet, which shows a variety of letterforms and sizes, plus additional characters, as well as the basic character set of each style. Type specimen sheets are used to promote and advertise typefaces that are sold commercially.

RESEARCH

Research is a systematic investigation into one or more aspects of a design project. It is an integral part of the design process because it is the only way to ensure that you are solving the correct problem, targeting the right audience, and not re-making what has been done before. On larger, long-term assignments, research may take up at least a third of the time a designer spends on the project. Research gives you information about the competition and what other designers have already produced in the category. It is used to provide a complete picture of the audience and to learn about the environment where the end result will be seen. Research isn't only for professional designers. Students should conduct research for every project they work on as well. Think about what might happen if you were to skip this step when designing a poster for a visiting designer who is giving a talk at your school. Time is short, so you create what you think is a pleasing design using one of your favorite typefaces. Information is clearly communicated, but unfortunately, unknown to you, the visiting designer is famous for creating typefaces using found objects. The poster with your favorite typeface seems out of place and isn't well matched to the subject. Both of these problems could have been easily avoided had you done a bit of research before you started laying out the type. Research does not have to be difficult, nor does it have to take a lot of time. Start by using Google or another search engine to do quick searches about the content or subject you are working on. Check to see what other designers have done with similar projects while being careful to avoid mimicking or copying their ideas. Later you will learn more advanced research techniques and how to apply these competencies to upper-level student projects and/or undergraduate thesis work.

above and right

Research into what has been done before and specifics of a product category helps designers know whether they are on the right track with their work. When creating the identity and labels for this craft brewery, the designers referenced history by using a crest but updated the look by using very modern elements within the outlines.

Design: Cast Iron Design, Boulder, Colorado

VISUAL DESIGN DEVELOPMENT

Design students often ask where concepts come from. As we discussed in Chapter 1, concepts are simply ideas. They are developed at the beginning of a project after research is complete and are based on the specifics of content you have to work with and the goals of the assignment. They are often rooted in visual/verbal associations, but they can also be based on a visual element in the design or even a single word or phrase. Some design projects are more suited to being concept-driven than others. Concepts are sometimes complex and recognizable by the viewer, but other times an idea will help a designer arrive at a novel solution that won't be identifiable to viewers. Advertisements, logos, and the packaging for a new product will benefit from strong concepts. On the other hand, the primary goal of instructional diagrams is to clearly convey information, and a simple solution using text and drawings might be most effective. Concepts are important regardless of whether the audience knows where they came from or can pick out a particular idea. In school, your work will be stronger if you are able to tie the visuals you create into a compelling idea. After school you will be expected to be able to highlight the concept or ideas behind the visual work when making presentations to clients.

Concepts can be overt and obvious or they may rely on a more subtle visually based system of arrangement and styling. For example, an advertisement could use a pun to promote a product, or the concept for a book design might be based on the verticality of the buildings described in the text. In the latter example, the audience will appreciate the connection between content and layout but may not be able to precisely identify the concepts behind it. Be on the lookout for opportunities to introduce a creative concept in every project. Just because you haven't communicated content using strong concepts in the past doesn't mean you can't do so now.

left

With an interesting concept and unusual visuals, this poster for the play Macbeth feels fresh and modern.

Design: Stephan Bundi, Boll, Switzerland

right

Concepts can be simple and rely on visual shapes more than on overt ideas. The placement of type mimics the form of the boat in the image and provides a subtle conceptual tie in between the type and image used in the design of this calendar.

Design: Marko Rašić & Vedrana Vrabec, Zagreb, Croatia

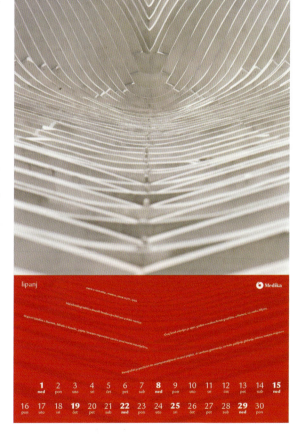

San Francisco–based Hatch worked with Krave Jerky founder Jonathan Sebastiani to develop a concept-based brand strategy that was then used for the visual identity, logo, product packaging, point-of-sale materials, advertising, and a website.

Background and Opportunity: A Jerky Revolution

The jerky category was stagnant and lacking innovative products and package design for decades. Krave was a new brand founded to bring a protein-loaded snack with artisanal flavors to athletes, busy moms, and health-conscious snackers. The brand strategy showcased Krave as a gourmet product exploding with personality.

Challenge

Hatch's challenge was to communicate a fresh approach to healthy snacking. Krave needed a visual identity and brand idea that would completely change perceptions from a convenience store and truck stop snack to a delicious and healthy snack for every day.

Audience

The designers learned as much about their audiences as possible. Kravers (the designers' name for the audience) have an on-the-go lifestyle. They train for marathons while juggling work and kids and socializing with friends. They often replace meals with better-for-you snacks, wanting a nutritional benefit and a satisfying, if not indulgent, flavor punch.

Research-based insights

- A new level of gourmet snacking: Consumers are reaching beyond the usual chips, crackers, and cookies to foods that have more healthful, satisfying benefits.

- Natural fuel that's fun and flavorful: Showcase the ingredients to amplify the mouth-watering, unique, and exotic flavor combinations and imbue the brand with a gourmet appetite.

- Krave fits your lifestyle: Whether you're a mom or dad packing lunches or taking snacks on the go, an athlete training for the next race, or a student studying for the big exam or socializing with friends, everything tastes better with Krave.

Impact of the design

Hatch's design and branding for Krave made the company a "disruptor brand," driving innovation with double-digit category growth for the first time in decades. In just two years, Krave could be found in 25,000 grocery stores, in specialty retailers, on Virgin flights, and in hotel mini bars. In 2013, the company's business grew over 300 percent. Krave became the #2 jerky brand in grocery in 2014, and USA Today called jerky "the new 'it' snack." With such a successful launch into mass retailers, Whole Foods asked Krave to create an exclusive line of premium flavors and packaging to match. In 2015 the candy and snack food giant Hershey's bought Krave.

"HATCH HAS DELIVERED AN ENTIRELY UNIQUE LOOK IN THE CATEGORY, RESULTING IN IMMEDIATE ADOPTION AT RETAIL—AND HAS PROPELLED OUR BRAND TOWARDS REALIZING OUR GOALS."

Jonathan Sebastiani (Founder & CEO, Krave)

JUMPSTARTING INSPIRATION

Ask a successful designer where his/her ideas come from and you might be surprised by the answer. Inspiration is unpredictable. One person will be inspired by the lyrics of her favorite song, another by the stories told to him as child, and a third by a great meal. There's no single recipe for producing good ideas because inspiration is nonlinear. It happens to different people at different times, for different reasons.

Have you had an idea come to you come out of the blue? Maybe it happened while you were on your way to class, while you washed dishes, or as you started to fall asleep at night. These moments of sudden insight are pretty typical. Even when our minds are at rest or distracted, they are still working to solve the problems we gave them earlier in the day or even a week before. You won't always be lucky enough to have ideas appear out of nowhere, so you need tools to jump-start idea generation. This section includes several methods for brainstorming and generating concepts. Each activity can be performed alone, or two or more systems can be combined.

below

Designers pride themselves on coming up with unusual ideas. Using tape to create the numbers and the background visual on the promotions for a summer arts camp is unexpected, but it makes the pieces feel original. Remember, even the best ideas need to be tested to ensure they work with the content and correctly target the audience.

Design: Sagenvier Design Kommunikation, Dornbin, Austria

REPEATING WHAT ALREADY EXISTS

Good concepts need a solid grounding. Ask yourself what is special, unique, and most important about the assignment. How have designers approached similar problems in the past, and what are the strengths and weaknesses of these solutions? Assessing what has been done previously will help you avoid predictable visual pairings. Your designs should have staying power and be memorable.

AVOID CLICHÉS

When an idea or visual pairing is used too often, it loses its freshness and becomes predictable. Clichés are common, but they don't belong in your design projects. Relying on what has been done before may feel more secure, but derivative ideas won't be as effective as original ones. To find a great concept you have to take risks. Try to identify any clichés associated with a topic and determine whether these approaches are effective or have limitations. Could something else work better? Is a fresh approach needed? If not, why have you been asked to solve the problem? What should the viewer do, learn, or feel? Answers to these questions provide a road map for concept development.

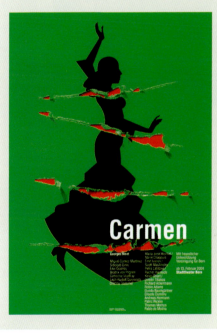

left

With what appears to be an actual tear in the paper on which the image is placed, this poster for the play *Carmen* avoids being a cliché or feeling too predictable. Avoiding clichés is particularly important when you are designing for well-known topics, stories, or plays like *Carmen*.

Design: Stephan Bundi, Boll, Switzerland

BRAINSTORMING AND IDEA DEVELOPMENT

Brainstorming is a structured activity used to develop creative solutions to a problem. It can be both visual and verbal. Some people use lists and diagrams to brainstorm, while others use sketches and images. This section includes several common brainstorming techniques that can be used to develop concepts for design projects.

FREE ASSOCIATION

Free association is a technique used to generate ideas. Begin by writing down facts about the project. Include goals, information from the brief or assignment, and a few details about the core values of the "client" or the information that needs to be conveyed.

Then make a list of words that pop into your head. Words should come spontaneously and be unedited. They don't need to relate to the project in any discernable way.

- Don't worry about whether the ideas will lead to a design solution. Instead, let your mind wander. At first you might think about what you ate for lunch, a snippet of a song, or the vacation you are planning with friends. Resist the urge to edit; this is free association.

- Spend at least ten to fifteen minutes working on your list of words. Keep the facts about the project visible, but don't worry too much about relating the ideas to the project. The goal is to get out of your comfort zone and find new ways of conceptualizing content.

- Most of what is produced during free association and sketching doesn't end up being used in final layouts. That's okay. The more words we produce the greater the chance that a unique concept will emerge. If some of the words immediately generate mental pictures you can make quick thumbnail sketches of your ideas.

Once you have completed your list you need to think about how the words might relate to the assignment. Identify ways each of the words or phrases can connect to the topic. Construct a mental image and then make quick sketches of those pictures. You should end up with several pages of rough sketches and notes.

- Don't worry about compositional details or drawing ability. Both will only slow you down.

- Some ideas will be more literal and others will be abstract.

- This process may produce additional words or phrases. Jot these down as well.

right

Brainstorming and idea development can produce a range of visual solutions. Some will be more successful than others, but as you begin to work on visual exploration, don't worry about which iterations "look the best"; instead, try to come up with as many ideas as possible. Quantity is a hallmark of good brainstorming, and these designers came up with many versions of the identity.

Design: Jessica Monteavaro Garbin and Fabricio Lima Dos Santos

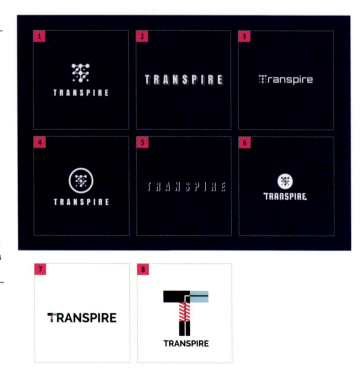

Take a break. It's best to wait at least a day to evaluate sketches, but when time is limited try to step away from your brainstorming for at least a couple of hours between sessions.

Now, it's time to review the design concept sketches. Evaluate how well each idea conveys the message. If you keep in mind the goals of the assignment, good ideas should stand out on the page. Choosing two or three of the best won't be difficult. Concepts are like ingredients that can be used to produce different dishes. A single concept can be applied to different size formats and even different design deliverables.

Once you have identified several potentially successful concepts, the next stage is to use type and images to visually express your idea. The principles of arrangement outlined in Chapter 7 will help you create balanced compositions. Not every concept will work as a finished design solution. Eliminate ideas that don't work and keep the ones that do. Consider using the ideas with actions from page 39 to explore different ways of thinking about content.

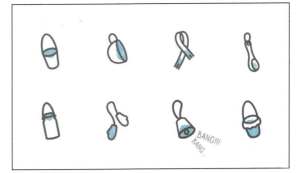

left

Drawings of items that are associated with cows and milking provide the concept for the designer to connect the brand name "milky land" with the different milk product sold by the client.

Design: Izyum Creative Group, Kiev, Ukraine

WAYS OF FRAMING THE DESIGN PROBLEM

These questions provide a lens to assess the goals of a project and to tease out specifics about what criteria will determine success.

- What is the viewer or user going to get out of the design?
- Who is the target audience?
- Does the design have a purpose?
- Should the tone be informational or persuasive?
- What would you want to see if you were the viewer/user?

REASONS NOT TO START A DESIGN DIGITALLY

- Your concepts are unlikely to be as original or experimental.
- You may focus on details too quickly.
- You may be influenced more by software tools than by the concept.
- Your layouts may seem stilted and predictable.

USING CONNECTIONS

If you get stuck on a project and don't know where to start, it can be useful to consider the principles below. Give yourself five or ten minutes to brainstorm using each of these modules. You can go back and develop ideas more fully later. Using a sketchbook or large notebook, list three goals for your project and make sketches for how each principle can be visually expressed. Don't worry about your drawing skills and don't create full layouts. This process is quick and dirty. You shouldn't spend more than a minute on each sketch. Some of your ideas will be visual; other ideas can be represented by words. If you use words, sketch a quick diagram so you will remember the idea later. Once you have finished the sketches for one category, start work on the next. After you have completed the sketches for each module, review all your ideas and mark the most interesting concepts. These thumbnails are the blueprints for the initial drafts of your project. Visual exploration will still be needed to fully resolve compositional issues and present information in the correct order.

Connection is used to show association or linkage. Connections can be either literal or contradictory. Other principles like distortion and exaggeration can also enhance visual connections.

> **Literal** connections occur when two items or elements are linked.

> **Contradiction** occurs when something does the opposite of what one expects.

Space/depth can activate a two-dimensional plane. These principles can form the basis for a design solution and provide visually engaging space in which text and image content may be placed. Create several iterations where some aspect of space or depth is highlighted, exaggerated, or distorted.

Surprise and play tap into a viewer's emotions and are most effective when combined with a narrative or story. They can occur in a specific area of a composition, or one or more of the visual elements may be substituted for another.

above

The image of a young man creates a literal connection to the text in this brochure and poster.

Design: Sagenvier Design Kommunikation, Dornbin, Austria

right

A photograph of cut paper and type activates the space and creates a sense of depth in this typographically based poster. Don't be afraid to use real objects or physical materials even for a flat design like a poster.

Design: Stephan Bundi, Boll, Switzerland

left

Look at the heads on these figures. Unexpected visual combinations and humor can add an element of surprise and make the design stand out. The designers had models wear masks, and the results are both memorable and humorous.

Design: Sagenvier Design Kommunikation, Dornbin, Austria

IDEAS WITH ACTIONS

When a design uses action to tell a story, the result is often more engaging. Using the same method of sketching described previously, create concepts based on three of the following verbs. As before, your sketches should take less than a minute. Try using a pen rather than a pencil. It will prevent you getting too finicky with your drawing.

Magnify	**Reduce**
Distort	**Simplify**
Exaggerate	**Reverse**
Repeat	**Rearrange**

left

These posters promoting Croatian for beginners use a playful exaggerated style of illustration to emphasize the concept.

Design: Bruketa&Zinic, Zagreb, Croatia

STORYTELLING AND NARRATIVE

Combining words and images that don't immediately look like they should go together can create new narratives. For example, juxtapose unrelated images with text that links them. The resulting combination can change the way a viewer responds to the images and interprets the message. This natural tendency to try to understand and interpret what we see can be used to aid visual storytelling, but it can also lead to content overload in cases where the viewer makes increasingly complex associations. The following literary devices originated in speech and writing but can be used to create visual associations and to develop narrative in designs as well.

USING METAPHORS AND SIMILES

A metaphor is a word or phrase that describes a subject using an unrelated idea or point of comparison to create new meaning. Metaphors use one idea or visual to stand for something else and should not be confused with similes where two dissimilar things are overtly compared.

A visual metaphor for life might be shown using images of a lighted window and a closed door, whereas a simile could be expressed by pairing a picture of a young woman and a rose. In the simile the comparison is direct: The young woman is like the rose. The metaphor of life, however, relies on both the lighted window and the closed door together to create a third, less literal meaning.

above

Storytelling can be direct or subtle. The designers of this brand identity and website used the visual attributes of the imagery and an identity based on lines and angles to make a connection between the concept for LISI, Austria's entry in solar decathlon competition and the idea of a modular design that can be placed anywhere.

Design: Pérezramerstorfer Studio, Vienna, Austria

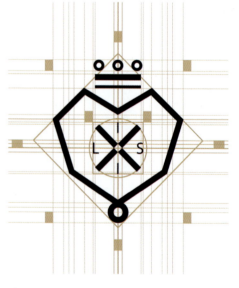

above

After a concept has been identified, it is still important to create a strong visual. Organizational structures like grids (see p. 197) can help you do so.

Design: Pérezramerstorfer Studio, Vienna, Austria

left

Penguins can't fit in ice cream cones, but this visual is the basis for a fun and light concept, which is perfect for collateral promoting a summer reading program.

Design: Sagenvier Design Kommunikation, Dornbin, Austria

below

The animated gif advertising a film archive makes use of personification with a character from the movie _Fantastic Mr. Fox_. The animation shows the fox's cape flapping.

Design: Pérezramerstorfer Studio, Vienna, Austria

PUNS

Puns rely on word play to suggest two or more meanings. They use words that have dual meanings or where similar-sounding words can stand in for each other. An example of a word pun is "broken puppets for sale; no strings attached." When used in design, an image may stand in for part or all of the word pairing.

PERSONIFICATION

Personification is also known as anthropomorphism. This is when aspects of human nature are applied to inanimate objects or animals. Personification is often used in advertising. Think of the GEICO gecko or the AFLAC duck. In each case the animal takes on human characteristics to present information about the company in a light-hearted, funny manner.

MATCHING OUTPUT TO AUDIENCE

Have you ever watched a commercial on TV and realized the visuals or tone of the advertisement was a complete mismatch with the people who are likely to buy the company's products? Sometimes in their zeal to be original and edgy, designers can lose their way and produce work that doesn't match the needs of the audience. The same thing can happen to student projects. The desire to make unique and engaging work can overshadow the realities of consumer preferences or the attributes of a particular age group. When this happens, your project will be unsuccessful regardless of how "cool" it looks, and you may have to abandon your design because it doesn't match the goals of the project. Letting go of a concept is hard, but it is a necessary part of the design process. If you do have to discard your first idea, keep it as a reference for future projects and evaluate why it failed to meet the objectives of the brief or assignment.

The more time you spend thinking about your target audience, the more likely you are to be able to produce appropriate visuals for them. Design students have a tendency to think about their audience too broadly. If you think your target is "everybody" or "everybody who can read," you have probably not been clear enough in your definition of the target. Start by asking questions and reviewing the goals of the project. Make notes and then try to develop a clear understanding of your audience.

What is the primary goal of the project?

- Is it informative?
- Does it ask the viewer to take action?
- Is it persuasive?

Who will realistically be viewing or using the end product?

- Are they young or old, male or female?
- What is their income?
- Do they drive a car or take public transportation?
- Are they interested in trying/buying new products or are they loyal to brands they already know?

By asking these questions you should start to be able to get a sense of who your audience is. Now you need to translate the information about your target into design decisions. Again, asking questions is helpful.

Will a particular visual style or the use of embellishments and imagery appeal to your audience?

- It is not enough for you and your friends to think a design is "cool." The design has to accomplish a particular task.

Does the age of your audience demand any special considerations?

- Older adults may require larger type for reading.
- Children favor bright colors and characters.
- Teenagers are likely to be interested in lively looking graphics.

---

below left

The target audience for this college view book app is prospective students and their parents. The design uses bright colors and lots of imagery to appeal to a young artistic audience and visually tell the story of California Collage of the Arts.

Design: Aufuldish & Warinner, San Anselmo, California

---

below right

Knowing that the audience will be more interested in images than words, the designers kept text to a minimum so viewers can scan through the pages and read small bits without becoming overwhelmed.

Design: Aufuldish & Warinner, San Anselmo, California

Does your audience have time to read a lot of text? If not, consider communicating primarily with visuals.

- In a busy environment it's easy to be overloaded with information. Imagery can reduce the need to read and act as a visual shortcut.

Do metaphors, puns or other visual/verbal devices offer any solutions that will appeal to your target?

- As we already learned, unusual or unexpected visual/ verbal pairings can extend meaning and provide emphasis.

It is often easier to design for people you have something in common with than it is to create visuals for a totally different population. As a professional designer you are likely to have to do both, so start practicing as a student. Remind fellow students and your instructor who you are trying to target when you show your work in critiques. Ask them whether they think your visuals match the audience.

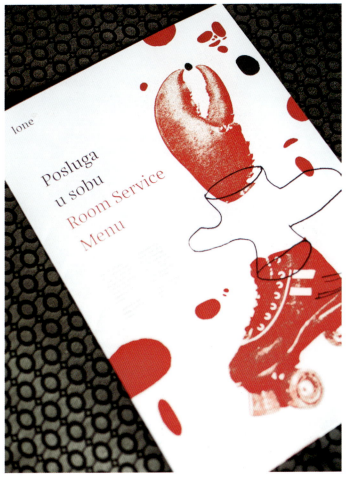

left
___

The concept for this upscale boutique hotel uses unusual images and odd juxtapositions to create a unique visual narrative about the company.

___

Design: Bruketa&Zinic, Zagreb, Croatia

above
___

Color and visual style help to unify all the pieces for Hotel Lone, and the juxtaposing of odd imagery targets a clientele who appreciate the unique feel of a boutique hotel.

___

Design: Bruketa&Zinic, Zagreb, Croatia

You Are Here Toledo (YAH) is a multimedia project that was inspired by a headline on Yahoo's home page, "The Most Miserable Cities in America," which featured the city of Toledo as the cover photo.

The goal: A resident of Northern Ohio, designer Jenn Stucker saw an opportunity for design to help engage visitors and the community. Instead of creating passive displays or banners, Stucker wanted to transform the citizen from viewer to participant and to share the rich history of the area. Through art and technology, the project provided social engagement for Toledo citizens and its visitors to discover the city and experience a new sense of community pride. Working with funding by local nonprofits and AIGA Toledo (AIGA is the premier professional organization for U.S. graphic designers, http://www.aiga.org) the project used a series of large, one-of-a-kind outdoor "dots" affixed to various public sidewalks throughout the city.

Collaboration: Northwest Ohio artists, designers, and students were asked to make a powerful visual statement in response to their assigned dot's location. One hundred dots marked the city, each containing a QR (quick response) code that allowed smartphone users to learn more about the artwork, its Toledo area location, and its local artist.

Participation: The project incorporated a scavenger hunt–like activity. Collecting and finding all 100 dots became a fun and interactive activity, which allowed viewers to discover information about the city. With a smartphone, the viewer could scan the QR code to unlock more contemporary and historical information about the dot's location and artist who created the dot artwork. The *You Are Here Toledo* project integrated mobile technology by developing a mobile app, made available through iTunes and Google Play, that allowed individuals to "check in" and log the dots they "collected."

Measuring success: Local residents and visitors embraced the project, and web and app analytics revealed 139 app downloads the first day (114 iOS, 25 Android), 832 total App downloads (472 iOS, 360 Android), 3,791 unique site visitors, 21,188 page views overall, and 8,597 dot detail page views from mobile devices. Returning users made up 45.65 percent of the site visits. More importantly, anecdotal feedback on Facebook included heartfelt thanks from participants who had fun learning more about the city of Toledo.

REVISION AND EXPERIMENTATION

Sometimes the first idea you have will end up being the best solution for a design, but most of the time you will need to work on several versions of an assignment before identifying the best solution. Even then, revision is necessary to fine-tune details like placement and the scale of typography. Exploring multiple ideas leads to better quality work. It also keeps you from using the same visual solution over and over. This system of revision and experimentation is not exclusive to design. Engineers, writers, and chefs use similar methods, respectively, to produce more efficient cars, award-winning novels, and delicious new recipes.

After one or more versions of a design have been developed, you will need to get advice from the client or your instructor on how well the design meets the intended goals of the project. Revision occurs after you have received feedback. Through a process of trial and error you will test and identify when the placement, color, and scale enhance the message and support the overall project objectives. Depending on the size of the project, a design may need several rounds of revision before an effective solution is produced.

This step-by-step approach also closely mimics the professional design process. Design companies typically present at least three versions or ideas of a design to the client. Even after an initial concept is chosen by the client, the designer will continue to create new variations of the layout before arriving at a version that most effectively solves the problem, engages the audience, and meets the project goals.

Regardless of whether you are working on school project or are employed by a client, the process of developing design solutions (sometimes called ideation) relies on a cycle of revision and feedback. Both the initial proposed design solutions and subsequent revisions are subject to feedback, and multiple versions of at least one concept are usually required before you will be able to produce the final design. This is a part of the workflow in professional practice and is a good one to employ as you are developing your own projects, whether for class or for personal reasons.

left, above and right

This student created multiple iterations of a label for a cleaning product aimed at men. Each design had its own concept, and during critique the student received feedback on what made some versions better than others.

Design: Jessica Monteavaro Garbin, New York

MAKING BETTER WORK FASTER

As stated previously, it is often necessary to revise project a number of times based on the feedback you receive during critiques or in discussions with professors. Using this working process you will eventually be able to recognize when one solution is more successful than the others. It also helps produce better work more quickly, which is key to making the transition from student to professional. As an advanced design student you may be required to produce a fully realized layout including type and image in the same amount of time or in even less time than you were given to develop initial ideas when you started your studies. By the time you graduate and become a professional designer, you will be expected to produce layouts and design ideas even more quickly, and you will also have to juggle working on more than one project at a time. School is a good place to practice these skills and prepare for the demands of fast-paced design jobs.

PRESENTING DESIGN WORK

Learning to present work to peers and potential employers is one of the most important skills a designer can master. At the start of a project, it may be acceptable to show sketches of preliminary ideas. But later, more fully realized computer-rendered layouts will be required, and toward the end of an assignment it is often necessary to produce a high-quality printed or three-dimensional version of the proposed designs for print-based work. We will learn more about production in Chapter 8, but it is important to keep the following production basics in mind as you study the principles discussed in the next few chapters.

Digital work and designs that are intended to be viewed on a screen should be presented on screen, and instructors will advise you whether to present working files or more finished digital comps. Showing well-thought-out concepts and visuals is always important, but craft shouldn't be overlooked. Craft is similar to neatness and refers to the how well a two- or three-dimensional item or printout is displayed or constructed. Craft is important to digital work as well. Make sure to have a clean art board (that's the space around the live design area) and a well-organized file. If multiple layers are used, consider showing a flattened file or naming the layers so you can easily make them visible and invisible if needed. As long as you maintain attention to detail, good craft can easily be achieved and will markedly improve how your design work is received in a critique setting.

above

The more designs you make, the faster you will become at learning what works and how to produce effective communications pieces.

Design: Katie Mias, New York

below

Creating volumetric renderings in Illustrator allows designers to show three-dimensional designs without having to physically produce the product. It is a great technique to use for client presentations.

Design: Elephant Design, Pune, India

above

When designing items using multiple materials, it is often necessary to test them first. You may need to create mock-ups by hand before sending a design out for printing/production. If you need to show mock-ups to the client or your instructor make sure they are neat and the craft is well done.

Design: &Larry, Singapore

PRESENTING WORK-IN-PROGRESS

Every project is different, and the requirements of an assignment vary depending on the facilities available and the type of project you are working on. Some projects are better suited to being printed, whereas others will be easier to critique on screen. Your instructor will tell you which method to use when presenting drafts of your projects.

Sketches: Detach from the sketchbook or notebook for easy viewing. Remove uneven edges with scissors or an X-Acto knife. Go over pencil lines with a black pen or marker so the drawings can be seen from a distance.

Printouts of in-progress work: Carefully trim white edges off paper with an X-Acto knife. If a layout includes extra white space around it, that space will be considered part of the design.

Printouts of final work: If possible, print on good quality, bright-white paper. Trim white edges off paper if they are not part of the composition. Depending on the requirements of the assignment, mount work on Foamcore or board (see p. 224). Make sure to paste/mount work onto the board before trimming the edges of the board.

Three-dimensional objects and multipage documents: Packaging and three-dimensional objects or signage can be shown as digital renderings or as fully produced mock-ups. When creating mock-ups, carefully construct three-dimensional designs so they are as neat as possible and make sure to protect them during transit. Construct multipage projects using high-quality paper and board. Consider using the "booklet" feature of Adobe InDesign or printing double-sided pages if signatures are needed. Three-dimensional objects and signage or other large-scale work can be digitally inserted in a photograph of real space to show how it could appear in a real-life setting.

Websites, motion graphics, user interface designs: Show work on screen. Test websites and motion graphics to ensure the images are rendered correctly, the audio is operational, and all of the links work. Unless otherwise stipulated in a project brief or assignment, design work should be presented in the same media used for the final output. For instance, websites and motion graphics should be shown digitally (usually by projecting the work onto a large pull-down screen or a monitor), whereas print design and packaging should be printed on paper and trimmed to size or put together (for packaging design) and made into a three-dimensional sample.

CRITIQUE AND ANALYSIS

The more time you spend looking at work, the easier it is to differentiate between effective aspects of a project and those that still need improvement. In-progress and final critiques are embedded in most project-based design classes, but the format for how a critique is conducted will vary depending on where you are studying and your instructor's preferences. The most common form of critique requires participants to display and talk about their work. Then the instructor and/or fellow students will give advice on how well the work has met the criteria outlined in the assignment. Sometimes the feedback will include proposals for how to develop specific aspects of a project, but other times the critique may focus almost exclusively on listing areas in need of revision. Critiques can also be conducted as one-on-one meetings or in small groups. Working in small groups allows students to practice giving each other more direct feedback, and in some cases fellow students may even make notes directly on your work similar to how an instructor would.

Critiques exist to help you improve your work. They also mimic the professional environment by simulating scenarios similar to those you might find in the workplace. At first it may be difficult to hear negative comments about your work. This is especially true when you have spent hours working on a particular piece or when you feel you have already come up with an innovative or unusual idea. Unfortunately, not all good ideas work well in all situations, and even great ideas may not be suitable for particular content or for a targeted audience. For example, you might come up with a great logo, but if it doesn't hold up visually when it is reduced to a smaller size, it can't be put on a business card. Similarly, the logo might feel too formal for use in package design, and you might need to go back and rethink the design. Sometimes great concepts fail to come together visually. You might have an idea to use an image of constellations in space as the background for packaging for a tech product. The connection between the concept and the content is great, but the visual might be too complex to work with the typography. In these instances, a total revision or new version of the project may be needed. It's important not to get discouraged by the critique process. Unrealized versions of a project are never a waste of time. Even if an idea isn't applicable to one project, it might be used on a future assignment. Keep castoffs for later by jotting the concepts down in a sketchpad or save a version of the original work in a flat file or a portable portfolio.

above

When creating three-dimensional objects, documentation is key to being able to show the final product in a portfolio. As a student, this often means producing a comp or mock-up specifically so you can photograph it in a real-world situation. The designers of this "inclusive watch" photographed the packaging alongside the brochure about the "product."

Design: Bruketa&Zinic, Zagreb, Croatia

EVALUATION AND ASSESSMENT

Just because a client has signed off on project or you received a grade doesn't mean the project is over. An evaluation needs to be conducted to assess what you learned from the project and to identify any areas you could have changed to achieve a more successful outcome. At the end of every project, you should consider whether the design achieved the goals originally described in the assignment and whether it correctly targeted the audience and was displayed well. A good concept goes a long way, but a project can still suffer from poor craft or problems with production. Be honest with yourself. By considering both the positive and negative aspects of your solution, you will be able to produce better work in the future.

STUDENT WORK GROUPS

Working on a project alongside fellow students can be a great way to develop a structured working process and solicit additional feedback. Start by identifying classmates who have similar interests. Then designate special times to meet and review one another's work. If computer labs are available, consider spending several hours working on a project in the lab with other students (you can also meet up and do the same thing working on laptops). Show each other work at regular intervals and allow time for comments. Giving constructive criticism gets easier with practice, so don't be discouraged if it feels awkward or not completely productive the first few times. Getting feedback from classmates who are working on the same project or upper-level students who are in the same program and who understand what you are trying to achieve is likely to provide useful and applicable feedback. Remember, we are almost always better at seeing mistakes or problems with someone else's work than we are with our own. That being said, it won't always be appropriate to incorporate all the advice you receive from classmates. If the feedback is similar to what you receive from your instructor, however, then the comments are probably on target.

above

Critiques offer the opportunity to present your work to others and to receive feedback from classmates and your instructor.

below

This identity required the designers to create multiple iterations before a final solution was chosen and implemented. In professional situations, members of the design team and the client usually give feedback on preliminary designs. In school you will receive feedback from classmates and your instructor.

Design: This is Folly, Minneapolis, Minnesota

TIPS FOR GIVING FEEDBACK

1. When you give positive feedback, be specific and avoid making more than three positive comments on a project. Instead of saying, "I like it," talk about the color, image, and type choice. For instance, you might say, "The imagery is particularly strong and draws my attention to the text content," or "The warm, bright colors are a good fit for the intended audience."

2. Always talk about the quality of the work and not the person. For example, you might say that the color a person has chosen isn't enhancing the type content, but it is inappropriate to tell a person he/she made a "bad or stupid choice" by picking a particular hue.

3. When evaluating a piece of design, be sure to consider the goals of a project and the population targeted by the message. It is easier to give constructive criticism when one has particular objectives to evaluate the work against. Avoid giving positive feedback for interesting visuals if they don't meet the intended goals of the project.

4. Evaluate the message of the design and decide whether the designer has styled the most important information in such a way as to be the first thing a person will see (for more on visual hierarchy, see p. 72). If not, tell the designer immediately. Great looking visuals cannot save a project if they don't clearly communicate content.

DISCUSSION POINTS TO PREPARE FOR CRITIQUES:

- Why is it necessary to produce multiple versions of a project?

- Why is feedback needed, and who should give it?

- How can one provide useful information to classmates working on the same project?

- How does one know when a solution is successful?

- How does the intended media for production and the target audience affect success?

- How can one criticize a person's work without criticizing someone personally?

- What should one do if one receives overly negative feedback?

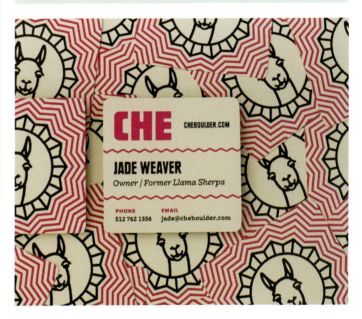

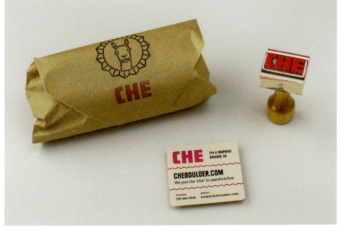

left

The text, graphics, and packaging reflect the zaniness and peculiar sense of humor present throughout the cafe. The designers purposely used a tagline that might win an award for one of the world's "worst": "We put the 'che' in sandwiches." The play on words is obviously dumb, but it is also memorable, a key attribute of any good tagline.

Design: Cast Iron Design, Boulder, Colorado

above

The owner of Cafe Che is an eccentric who brings his enthusiasm and personality to every aspect of the cafe.

Design: Cast Iron Design, Boulder, Colorado

EXERCISE:
Book covers/online advertising
Courtesy of Liz DeLuna

Part 1: Research

Read one of the following two books. Using an online search engine, look for book reviews and other information about the author and the content of the book.

The Learners by Chip Kidd

Mr. Penumbra's 24-Hour Bookstore by Robin Sloan

Part 2: Brainstorming

Make a list of the most important ideas in the book. Consider the tone, the historical and cultural context, and whether the content offers opportunities to use puns or metaphors. Then use one or more of the brainstorming techniques outlined earlier in the chapter to create original concepts for your designs.

Part 3: Visual exploration

Create two versions of a book cover using combinations of type and imagery. For one version develop your own imagery using one of the techniques detailed in Chapter 6. The imagery can be photographic, illustrative, or based on a fine art technique like collage or painting.

Specifications:

Print: Dimensions: 5 × 8 inches front only. Double the size to 10 × 8 inches and add space for the spine for the final presentation.

Content: The cover must include the author's name, the title, and any other text from the "real" book cover (both front and back).

Presentation: Print your covers and trim the printout to the final size of the book. Locate two books that are roughly 5 × 8 inches and put the final covers on the actual books for critique. Note: You may need to amend the size of your designs slightly to fit around the books.

Digital: Design the book cover at 5 × 8 inches for the front and for the back cover. The cover must include the author's name, the title, and any other text from the "real" book cover (both front and back). Next, scale your design to 260 × 480 pixels and evaluate whether the cover holds up well at the new, smaller size. Mock up your design using a screenshot of the book's actual Barnes & Noble or Amazon page.

Optional Digital: Create a leader board and rectangular advertisement to promote the book using some of the elements from your cover design. The designs should be complementary so they can be seen together on the same site/page.

Leader board: 728 × 90 pixels

Large rectangle: 336 × 280 pixels

Half page: 300 × 600 pixels

CHAPTER IN REVIEW:
Do's and don'ts

1. Review the steps in the design process and create specific design-related goals for the project. (pp. 28 and 46)

2. Use visual exploration and ideation to create unique design solutions. (p. 46)

3. Always begin a project with research. (p. 32)

4. Avoid clichéd subject matter and overused visual/verbal associations like unicorns, hearts, or any other subject that looks like it belongs on a greeting card (unless you are designing greeting cards). (p. 35)

5. Use brainstorming exercises and sketching to develop a concept for how you will solve the visual and conceptual problems of the assignment. (pp. 36–41)

6. When appropriate, use storytelling to create compelling visual narratives. (p. 40)

7. Match your design solution to the target audience. (p. 42)

8. Create a working group with other students so you can get feedback on projects while they are in progress. (p. 50)

9. Ask for feedback on how well your design is targeting the audience and communicating information from your instructor and peers. (p. 50)

10. Before presenting work, review the fundamentals of presenting and critiquing work. (p. 51)

Chapter 3 / Form and Space

CHAPTER 3:
Form and Space

KEY TERMS AND CONCEPTS:

Active or Activating refers to literal or implied movement in design. Activating part of a design or a composition means to consider all areas of the page or live area and to place elements so the space is balanced and individual elements maintain hierarchy. An active design is generally considered better than one that is static. (p. 66)

Bleed is the area outside the trim of a page or live space. The term originally comes from printing terminology but is now used when referring to screen-based design as well. If you are asked to bleed something off a page it means that the element should extend beyond the edge of the page. (p. 76)

Composition, or compositional space, is the area where layout or design occurs. (p. 59)

Contrast occurs when two things are different from each other. Scale, color, and style can all produce contrast. (p. 79)

Cropping is removal of parts of an image or other element to improve the framing of a single element or an overall composition. (p. 58)

Element is an item such as a line, type, or image that exists within a composition. (p. 56) (Also see *form* and *figure*.)

Figure is another word for *form*. The front or foreground of a composition is made up of elements, or forms. Behind the forms is the ground, background, or negative space. (Also see *form*.) (p. 70)

Figure-ground refers to the relationship between the form or imagery and the background also known as the negative space. Variables like contrast, value and scale may affect how distinct the form appears in relationship to the ground. (p. 70)

Form refers to any element in a design. Images, type, and even dots or lines are all form. (Also see figure and element.) (p. 56)

Format refers to the proportions, size, or orientation of a composition or live area. (p. 59)

Ground (or background) is like negative space. It is an area of space without elements or form. (p. 58)

Hierarchy is the relative importance of elements within a composition. (p. 72)

Live area is the space in which a design exists. The term is primarily used when referring to screen-based design such as websites, app designs, or motion graphics. (p. 59)

Negative space is the space around visual elements. (See *figure ground*.) (p. 70)

Scale is the relative size of an item in a design composition. The term can be used as a verb as in "to scale" an image. (p. 74)

Static is lacking in movement or action. In design a space or element that is static is considered less interesting and generally undesirable. (p. 73)

VISUAL UNDERSTANDING

FORM

Viewers inherently look for meaning in visual material. If you draw a circle and a line on a blank page and show it to a friend, he/she will quickly start associating the shape with ideas. People have a natural tendency to look for meaning, and this is one of the reasons graphic design is such a successful medium for conveying information. This chapter identifies the formal elements most often used in design and examines how variables such as scale, balance, and repetition can be used to alter how forms are perceived and how they can be used in layouts.

At its very essence, design is produced by placing visual elements in either physical or virtual space. Basic elements in design are called "formal elements," and they include points, lines, patterns, and shapes. These "forms," or formal elements, can be combined to create an infinite number of visual arrangements. They can also be paired with more complex visuals such as images and type. You can change how formal elements behave in a composition by applying visual variables like contrast, scale, texture, and value and by placing them nearer to or farther from other elements. The combination of formal elements and visual variables can be used to set a mood, denote emphasis, and organize space. While it may be tempting to dive right in and begin working with type and image, it is worth the effort to spend time mastering the use of basic formal elements. This chapter is dedicated to examining the attributes of formal elements and the visual variables that affect how they behave in compositional space.

right

These compositions show the relationship between form and space. The placement of simple forms indicates depth and creates engaging visual space. By moving elements around, it is possible to create new compositions from the same basic elements.

Design: Acme, Paris, France

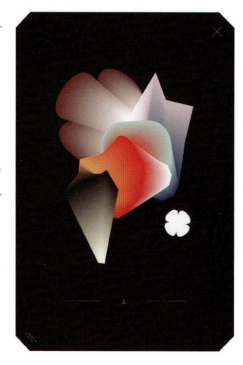
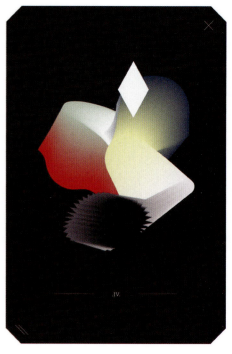

LOGO ELEMENTS

left

Simple forms like shapes and lines have versatility and are often used as the basis for identity marks.

right

When visual variables like color and texture are added they change how shapes are perceived. Notice how different the "box" looks when it has grass texture and wood grain added to the surface.

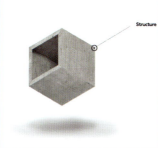

above

Here the identity is combined with dots and planes of color and is used as a splash screen for the company's app.

right

One of the benefits of working with shapes and lines is that they can be altered for some applications. Color can provide unity even when the shape of a form changes.

SPACE

Space can be defined as the area or context in which visual elements are placed. As each form is added, the relationship between design elements and the background is changed and an increasingly complex language of visual association develops. The interplay between visual elements, the meaning of content, and the compositional space creates the underlying basis for design layouts. Changing the order or placement of elements affects emphasis and provides variety within a live area or the designated compositional space.

SPACE AND VOLUME

The ground or space on which designers place elements often has no real, physical volume. Pages in books, websites, and applications exist in two- rather than three-dimensional space. When applied to otherwise flat forms, effects such as shading, shadow, texture, cropping, and gradation of tone can give the appearance of depth. Similarly, linear perspective and the placement of larger items in front of smaller ones will give the illusion of space because large objects appear closer to the viewer while smaller objects recede.

Carefully choosing the value (or the lightness or darkness of the color) of elements will also affect how objects are seen in relation to space. For example, darker elements or objects generally appear to be behind lighter ones and will be noticed after them. By using this principle you can control what a viewer sees first, second, and third and develop a sense of depth within the composition.

left

Space can be physical as in a location or object, or it can be produced by illusions created by the placement of elements within a design. This design relies on the illusion of depth derived from clouds that seem almost three-dimensional.

Design: Gerwin Schmidt, Munich, Germany

above

Lines of type, individual characters, and imagery create a sense of depth in this layout. The audience knows that the figure and the horizon of the edge of the earth couldn't really exist in the same space, but the composition is more interesting because the illusion of depth.

Design: Cheah Wei Chun, CLANHOUSE, Singapore

above

The compositional space in this series is activated by using repeated abstract forms in the background. This technique can be particularly successful when working with elements in time such as animated gifs, animated advertisements, or motion graphics.

Design Studio Beuro, East Sussex, United Kingdom

above

While much of the space used by graphic designers is implied rather than physical, there are designers who work to create engaging physical spaces like this library where even the ceilings and walls are considered part of the compositional space.

Design: Kuhlmann Leavitt, St. Louis, Missouri

LIVE AREA, COMPOSITION, AND FORMAT

The terms live area, composition, and format are all used to describe the space in which design occurs. Live area tends to apply to screen-based design, whereas composition is used more frequently when working in print design. Format refers to the proportions or size of a composition; for example, you might be asked to change the format by enlarging or reducing the overall size.

COMPOSITIONAL SPACE

The area in which visuals and content are presented is often referred to as the format, or compositional space. The size and shape of this space will affect how we perceive the visual and textual information. A large space can swallow up smaller elements and make them seem diminutive, whereas large forms can overpower a smaller space. When designing multipage documents like books, simple formal elements like lines, circles, or squares can create a sense of continuity and pacing among pages. Similarly, websites often use a combination of rectangles and lines to separate virtual space and usually provide a system of visual markers, such as arrows, to help users navigate through the information and between sections/pages. In packaging, shapes and lines are used to develop framing devices and spatial structure. As a designer, it is your job to control and organize both form and space so that the message you are trying to get across is clear and appropriate. Poorly arranged space can cause confusion or give importance to the wrong content. Too much space and a composition will seem empty and the elements will be weak. Too little space and a composition becomes over-crowded and confusing.

PRINCIPLES AFFECTING FORM AND SPACE

The *concept* is the expression of an idea. Designers use a combination of cognitive processes, visual experimentation, and interpretation to connect concepts with meaning and formal elements.

The term *content* refers to the underlying message or text communicated by the form. Depending on the nature of a project, content will be informational or it may seek to motivate a user to take a particular action. Form has content or meaning by itself, but when it is combined with text it will more directly convey information. As a designer considers pairing content and form, he/she needs to be aware of past precedent and create situations where the concept is well connected to the form.

The *context* refers to the external or virtual environment where a design will be seen. Designers need to recognize and respond to the physical context of a design and assess how these individual scenarios may affect how content is understood.

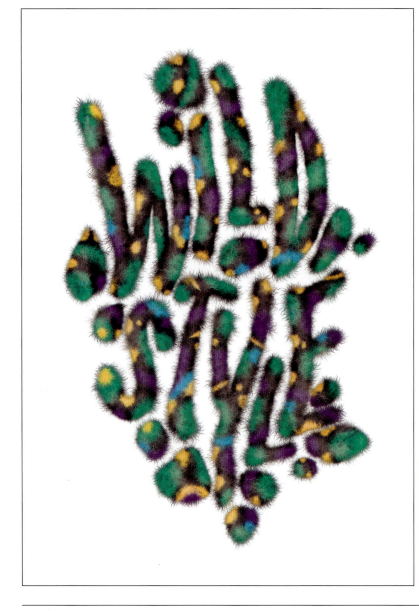

left

Concepts can be more or less literal. The concept wild is expressed very literally in this composition of type.

Design: Victor Bregante, Sitges, Spain

left

This poster uses a recognizable image of Darth Vader. The image is well matched to the content/ message because the poster advertises a film archive.

Design: Pérezramerstorfer Studio, Vienna, Austria

right

There are a lot of stimuli to compete with on the street. By using simple visual forms like arrows and a bright blue color, this poster stands out against the buildings around it which is the context in which the design lives.

Design: Project Projects, New York

Either overt or subtle, the underlying *structure* of a layout will determine how form exists in space and in relation to other elements in the composition. Grids are an example of one organizational method used in design, but the pairing of value, the style of photographs and illustration, and any other unifying principle also provides visual structure.

The *mode* is the visual style used to create a form. Form can be rendered using expressive techniques such as painting, drawing, or photography, or can it can be produced with simple lines and shapes. The visual style of form will affect both the explicit and associated meaning ascribed to a design.

In addition to being differentiated by visual appearance, form can be divided into unique expressions such as those created by hand for one-time use versus forms that already exist. Ready-made expressions of form include fonts, clip art, stock images, and illustrations. Customized forms have the benefit of specificity, whereas ready-made visual material is often appropriate when less precise visual associations are desirable.

above

The continuity of type, line, and image creates a structure for the design of this coffee packaging. Without structural elements like lines, the other elements in this design would have felt like they were floating and disorganized.

Design: Dedica Group, New York

Line Art | Drawing | Photo

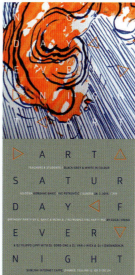

above

These compositions use different modes of imagery, including photography, painting, illustration, and collage.

Design: Marko Rašić & Vedrana Vrabec, Zagreb, Croatia

right

Ready-made props can feel unique when they are placed within a specific composition, as was done for this album cover. One usually has to photograph objects or ready-mades before using them in a design.

Design: Felipe Taborda, Rio de Janeiro, Brazil

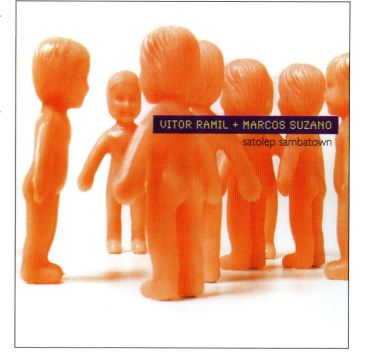

ELEMENTS AND ORGANIZATION

Points, lines, and shapes are the most basic elements for expressing ideas in graphic design. These abstract forms can be geometric or organic, big or small. By using these elements in combination, you can create an infinite array of visual solutions that are applicable to almost every type of graphic design project.

Using abstract forms is an excellent way to communicate concepts that are too complicated to be expressed with photographic imagery or when there is no good image match. Elements are found ready-made in most computer software but can also be created using a variety of art-making techniques. They can be produced quickly, and cheaply, since it is possible to create basic forms either with computer software or with analog methods such as drawing or painting. Simple elements tend to work well when paired with strong typography and may be used as either primary or supporting features in a composition.

POINT

A point is an exact position on a plane or in space. In their purest form, points exist without mass, but when a point acquires mass or when it is marked in some way, it becomes a dot. Dots create areas of focus. They are most often associated with small, round shapes, but the shape and size of dots can vary; they can be squares, triangles, spots of paint, or even photographs and objects. As soon as you introduce a point into a composition it changes the space. Add a second and third dot to a composition and you have the beginnings of a story. Adding more elements like dots to a composition will affect how each element is perceived. You can alter hierarchy by changing their order, placement, or color.

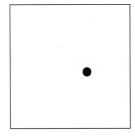
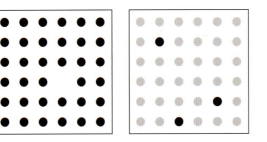

above

As soon as you introduce a point into a composition it changes the space. Add a second and third dot and you can alter hierarchy by changing the order of the dots.

right

Consider using simple shapes as primary elements in a project where you don't want the visual specificity of images. Points are enlarged to become circles, and they create the basis for this identity design.

Design: Anagrama, Nuevo Leon, Mexico

LINE

A line refers to the space between two points. In their most basic form, lines have length but no breadth. Essentially a connective element, lines can be visible or invisible. Lines can also be implied, as is the case when two or more elements are placed next to each other in a row. A series of dots will be perceived as a line, as will a string of words. Since lines are connectors, they tend to be dynamic and are used to convey movement, separate space, provide emphasis, and denote boundaries by framing other elements. When they intersect with each other, the point of intersection immediately creates a focal point or area of heightened visual interest.

The quality of a line and the mode in which it is represented are as varied as its use. Lines are expressive and can be thick or thin, straight or curvy. They can be made using analog or digital techniques and are used to create shapes like circles and squares and even complex illustrations and letterforms. Changing the weight of a line alters how it is perceived. Thick lines have more visual weight than thin ones. When lines become very thick they may be seen as shapes or a flat plane. Perception is relative, so elongating a thick line will make it seem lighter or less weighty in a composition.

When repeated or rotated on an axis, lines create textures and alternative surface patterns. As with any element there should be a reason to include lines in a composition. Avoid adding lines to "fill up space," and if lines are used as a primary visual element in a composition, try a version with fewer or no lines and then add lines as needed to support the compositional goals and to help express specific content.

DIGITAL FORM-MAKING: LINES

Computer software re-creates gestures previously produced by the hand; many lines used by designers now originate in a computer program and are "drawn" with a stylus or created using tools like the line tool, pencil tool, or pen tool. Digital tools often reference analog production and materials. The gestural quality of digital mark and how much it references a handmade aesthetic changes depending on which tools are used.

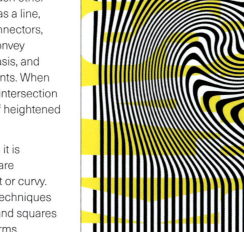

left

By making lines change from narrow to thick, the designer has created an optical illusion that is abstract and provides the focus of this eye-catching poster. The designer relies on the imagery to catch viewers' attention and draw them forward to read the small text.

Design: Goetz Gramlich, Heidelberg, Germany

above

Horizontal lines are restful, whereas angular lines have more tension and squiggly lines suggest movement.

WHERE LINES ARE USED IN DESIGN:

- As organizational structure
- Frames for photos or text
- To provide emphasis
- As independent compositional elements
- To create texture or patterns
- To create letterforms or shapes
- To create illustrations

PLANE

A plane is a flat, two-dimensional space. Depending on their form, planes can be regular or irregular. Dots and lines become planes when their size increases relative to the compositional space around them. Planes are used to provide emphasis and to separate the space in which elements are placed. As with other elements, the relationship between positive and negative space will affect the viewer's perception of a plane. When the sides of a plane are indicated, the object becomes a shape.

SHAPES

Flat objects defined by lines within a two-dimensional space are called shapes. Lines provide the boundary of the shape regardless of whether they are visible or invisible, smooth or rough. The most common shapes are circles, squares, and triangles, and each of these forms comes in a variety of sizes and proportions. One way to classify shapes is based on whether they have geometric or organic attributes. Geometric shapes are most often associated with man-made objects and usually have hard or regularly formed edges, whereas organic shapes refer to the natural world. Shapes are also differentiated depending on the technique used to create them and whether their edges are smooth or rough. For example, if you draw a triangle using the line tool on the computer, it will have a smooth, regular appearance that is quite different from if the same shape is made using a paintbrush. Depending on how they are rendered and what attributes have been applied to them, shapes can appear to be three-dimensional even while existing on a two-dimensional, flat plane or in digital/virtual space.

In a composition or live area, shapes are used as separate visual elements and to organize space. They can stand in for ideas and create patterns. You can also use shapes instead of a photo or illustration. When organizing space in a layout, clusters of shapes will add emphasis. Relative size, complexity, and other attributes like color and value have an impact on the overall appearance and visual weight of a shape.

Active versus passive: The following attributes can be mitigated by the relative placement of elements within the composition.

- Horizontal rectangles are usually more passive

- Vertical rectangles are considered to be more active spaces

right

When they are enlarged, dots become a plane. Planes can also be either regular or irregular shaped.

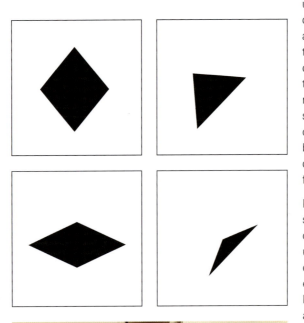

right

The compositional space in this poster is made more engaging with planes of different color. Consider using large planes or shapes in the background of compositions with only a few visual elements.

Design: &Larry, Singapore

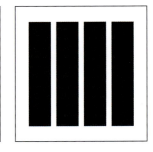

left

In this poster, shapes are used to organize space and provide different compositional areas where type can be placed. The pattern created by the black rectangles becomes the basis for the entire composition.

Design: Dan Lemperle, New York

left

By oddly cropping the image in this poster, the designer has created a composition showing two heads. One appears in the photo and the other is produced by the shape of the cropping.

Design: Stephan Bundi, Boll, Switzerland

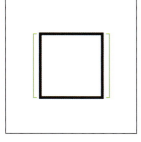
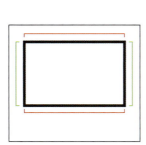

above

Putting a black rectangle behind a piece of white text will make it stand out and will separate it from other elements.

below

Squares have equal sides. Rectangles have two pairs of sides of equal length.

SHAPES CAN BE USED

- In place of images

- To emphasize content

- To help create organizational structures

- To direct a viewer's eye to break up a composition

- As part of illustrations or patterns

Simple shapes and color can be used to represent quantity and comparison when designing infographics. Shapes can also be used as a container for other elements such as type.

Design: Sonsoles Llorens, Barcelona, Spain

DIGITAL FORM-MAKING: SHAPES

In vector software like Adobe Illustrator, a shape consists of both an outline (also called the stroke) and the fill. Shapes can be altered or otherwise skewed by moving the position of the points used to create the shape. Digital shapes can be solid or opaque. They can also be layered on top of one another or have imagery or textures inserted as fill.

BEZIER CURVES

Lines are typically distinguished by whether they are straight or curved. Computer software includes tools for rendering both types of lines, but straight lines are easier to draw because they are made using techniques that mimic the natural motion of the hand. Since the lines found in computer programs are produced using mathematical equations, the process of rendering curves on the computer is more complicated than producing straight lines. Bezier curves use a mathematical equation to describe the trajectory or parameter of a curve based on the two end points. In vector graphics, Bezier curves are used to create smooth curved "paths" because they are infinitely scalable. They are also used to control or map out time-based motion when animating objects with key frames, and they can produce some of the shapes needed to design letterforms. In graphics software like Adobe Illustrator and Photoshop, Bezier curves are primarily produced using the the pen tool. Unlike the pencil or line tool, the way the designer controls the pen tool is non-intuitive and must be practiced. One begins by clicking to position points one after the other. Then the software program will interpret the space between the two points and form a curve. Handles allow the user to change the angle of the resulting curve, and keyboard shortcuts such as <shift> or <alt> allow a user to make segments of a line thicker or thinner. By "drawing" with the pen tool it is possible to represent most two-dimensional shapes. This technique is easily mastered by tracing an existing example of line art using the pen tool in Adobe Illustrator.

Bezier curves are used to create the following:

- letterforms
- type on a path
- complex shapes
- illustrations

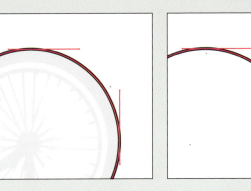
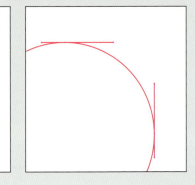

TEXTURE AND PATTERN

Texture is the appearance or feel of a surface. Textures can be hard or smooth, handmade or digitally rendered. When textures are added to a design they can be produced either by changing the material on which a composition is printed or by incorporating images of objects with a tangible quality. Images, paintings, and prints all have their own texture. In design, textures are most often used to add a tactile quality to two-dimensional space, to alter the surface quality of a project, to add detail, or to suggest a handmade effect. They can also act as visual shorthand to connect content to concepts or to create the illusion of physical space in a virtual environment. Both the surface of a physical object and an optically produced texture can give an element or even an entire layout a very different feel. Printed pieces often include texture as a way to set a mood or to enhance a surface, while in digital projects texture creates virtual depth or may provide a reference to the physical world.

In print-based work, you always have to consider the tactile nature of the paper and ink. Choosing a textured paper stock will affect the way that the final product looks as well as feels, and a textured stock will absorb ink differently than a smooth or glossy paper stock. The application of finishing processes like an aqueous (clear) coating or using embossing also affects the end result. Images and text look different depending on what type of paper they are printed on. Magazines like *Time*, *Newsweek*, and *Vogue* are usually printed on glossy paper, as is most packaging. Matte paper is more often used for art books, textbooks, or invitations. There is no absolute rule about when to use each type of paper stock. Instead you will need to assess the goals of the project and decide which option will best convey the information. Whether used online or in print, texture is an excellent tool to add value and to enhance meaning, but it shouldn't get in the way of readability.

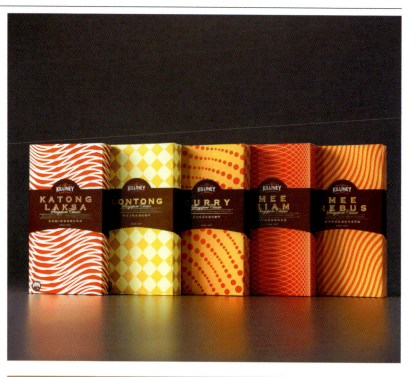

above

Colorful patterns make the rectangular form more interesting and differentiate each item in the series of classic Singaporean dishes.

Design: &Larry, Singapore

left

Texture can be physical or digital. Debossing (see p. 209) and a heavy matte paper provide physical texture for these business cards.

Design: Cast Iron Design, Boulder, Colorado

VISUAL VARIABLES

Having identified and described the formal design elements, in this next section we will explore how these attributes and simple organizational principles can be used to alter elements and to change their role within a composition. When considering the characteristics of form, such as value, texture, and scale, it is helpful to begin by analyzing which elements stand out the most in a composition (see hierarchy on p. 72). What is it about the placement of an element or its appearance that draws your attention to it? Is it the size? For example, a large object may have greater visual weight than other elements of the design. But a bright color might make a smaller element stand out in another situation. Examining how visual variables and organizational structures affect design compositions provides the groundwork to help you understand how to use these properties effectively in design projects.

FIGURE-GROUND

Form represents positive space, whereas the absence of form is called negative space. Negative space is also known as the ground (or sometimes the background or white space), and form refers to the figure. Figure-ground relationships are a mainstay of design. Form and ground are equally important, and they are interdependent. It is a mistake to concentrate exclusively on form. Attention to form without consideration of the ground will result in static, one-dimensional compositions, as will instances where the foreground and background of a composition have equal visual weight. Variation or contrast between the foreground and background creates more dynamic spaces and provides focal points, which increase visual interest. For example, in an overly crowded room it is almost impossible to pick out a particular person, but in a room with only one or two people, an individual stands out and becomes easily recognizable. Too much form and the composition becomes like the example of the crowded room; too little form and elements can get lost, and it is difficult to achieve the hierarchy needed to command a viewer's attention. At a minimum, figure-ground relationships should enhance rather than detract from a viewer's ability to understand visual order.

You can also reverse the figure-ground relationship by consciously switching the emphasis between the form and the ground. Elements can be seen as the ground, or the ground can become figure. An optical illusion can be created when the foreground and background are deliberately reversed or made ambiguous, causing the eye to shift from one image to the other.

left

The background of this digital poster changes in each frame. Texture and value are used to create continuity, whereas scale shows difference and indicates hierarchy.

Design: Acme, Paris, France

above

This example shows figure-ground relationships and figure-ground reversal.

USING POSITIVE AND NEGATIVE SPACE

As we have discussed, negative space comprises areas of a composition around or between visual elements, whereas positive space refers to the space taken up by elements such as text, image, or other expressions of form. Don't feel that you have to fill up space in order to make a composition feel more designed. Overcrowding can interfere with hierarchy and reduces visual interest. Effective use of negative space is one of the best ways to create emphasis and enhance text and image content.

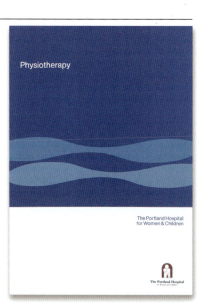

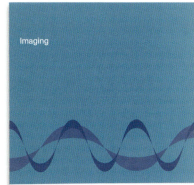

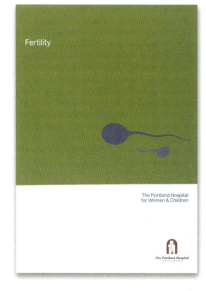

left

This poster plays with the idea of foreground and background. The background becomes part of the foreground when the face of the figure is left blank.

Design: Marko Rašić & Vedrana Vrabec, Zagreb, Croatia

left

The figure-ground relationship is somewhat ambiguous as the receding space in the image can be seen as either positive or negative. Using negative space in unusual or unexpected ways can draw attention to your design.

Design: Felipe Taborda, Rio de Janeiro, Brazil

above

This poster series shows how compositions with a lot of negative space can be just as engaging as ones where the space is filled with content. When working with only a few elements it is often helpful to reverse positive and negative space by switching the colors. If the composition works both ways, then both positive and negative space are well activated.

Design: Rebecca Foster Design, Birmingham, United Kingdom

HIERARCHY

Hierarchy is a visual logic used to achieve clarity of message. The term describes how elements relate to each other and are given prominence within a compositional space. All elements are interdependent, and hierarchy is largely determined by their visual weight and placement. Meaning and emphasis can be changed depending on the ordering of information and how visual variables such as scale, proximity, color, and value are used. Designers strive to make content clear and to create visual scenarios where users instinctively move through printed or digital material. Sometimes unsuccessful compositions simply lack hierarchy, while in other situations the use of placement or form may impede understanding. Ignoring rational hierarchy causes confusion or uneasiness for viewers.

BALANCE

The principle behind balance is gravity. Think of a scale or a seesaw at a playground. When a heavier item is placed on one side, the other side will rise. In graphic design, balance is used to create harmonious compositions and is visual rather than physical: "visually heavy" objects draw a viewer's attention to one side of a page or to an area in space. Smaller or lighter objects command less attention, and unless they are made more noticeable with a variable such as color, they will be seen after the "heavy" elements. Visual balance occurs when one or more elements are placed so that they have the same visual weight as the other elements in the composition. Designers usually strive for equilibrium within a given space, but since there are different ways of achieving visual balance, this goal is not as linear as you might think. Placement and proximity as well as variables like weight, scale, color, value, and texture can all be used to create a balanced composition. An unbalanced design will make viewers feel uneasy even if they are not able to describe why or what is out of place. Activating space with focal points and maintaining hierarchy will allow the designer to achieve balance while providing continual visual interest.

above

This poster series uses scale and placement to indicate hierarchy. The centered composition leads the eye to the middle of the page, and the large type stands out so the viewer knows what to read first. Try using scale to convey hierarchy in your own designs.

Design: Cast Iron Design, Boulder, Colorado

right

Consider using color to balance a composition. Half sheets of pink paper provide balance and offset the images of high-end lights in this promotional brochure.

Design: Lotta Nieminen, New York

SYMMETRY VERSUS ASYMMETRY

Compositions can be either symmetrical or asymmetrical, and both of these organizational systems can be used to achieve visual balance. Symmetrical compositions are based on pure equilibrium where elements strictly mirror each other on a central axis. True symmetry means that both right and left as well as top and bottom mirror each other, and it is most often used to create repetitive patterns. We tend to be more familiar with symmetry that exists on a vertical axis; the most common type of symmetry occurs when the left and right side of a composition look like the other. Symmetry is ordered and balanced, but it is a somewhat static way of organizing content. Title pages, poetry, and wedding invitations are associated with symmetry. This was the standard method for organizing content until the early part of the twentieth century.

Any time an element is placed off center without a corresponding element on the opposite side of the axis, a composition becomes asymmetrical. Asymmetry emerged out of the modern movement in the 1920s and '30s in Germany. At the Bauhaus, artists and designers experimented with creating off-centered compositions and angling the axis on which content was placed. The goal of contemporary design projects is rarely to achieve absolute balance or symmetry; instead the designer works to develop overall visual balance where elements play off of each other, creating focal points and areas of visual interest. Since symmetry produces more static compositions, it is easier to communicate complex messages using asymmetry, and today most designers develop balanced designs using variations on this system.

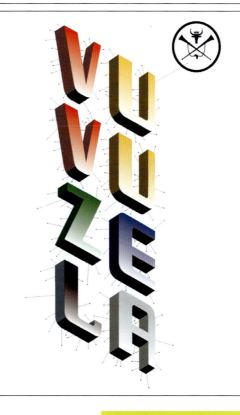

left and below

These two pieces by the South African designer Garth Walker show very different approaches to layout. One is symmetrical, and the other is asymmetrical. The asymmetrical layout (shown on the left) is balanced by the element on the top right, whereas color helps to balance the symmetrical layout while maintaining visual interest in the bottom composition.

Design: Garth Walker, Durbin, South Africa

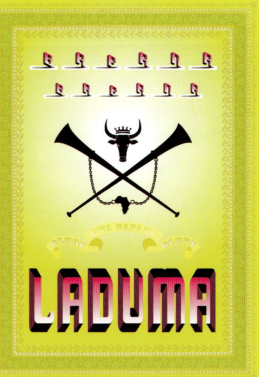

left

Contrary to what you might think, symmetry is often more difficult to work with than asymmetry. To use symmetry successfully, it is often best to keep a symmetrical design simple and only use a few visual elements. These posters rely on a symmetrical layout to arrange the visual elements. The interplay of bright colors and shapes keeps the compositions from feeling static.

Design: THERE, Surry Hill, Australia

SCALE

The term "scale" is used to denote the size of an object or the graduated ordering of separate elements. Scale is relative, and the perceived size of one element will be dependent on the size of the objects around it and the ground, or live area, in which it exists. When the term is used to describe the relational sizing of elements in a composition it is called hierarchy, and this type of scaling is important when designing with type and ordering elements in a layout. For more information on hierarchy see page 72. Scale can be used to provide contrast or, when multiple elements are scaled in relation to each other, it will create a sense of rhythm or the appearance of movement. When all of the elements in a composition have a similar mass and dimension, there is nothing to draw the eye, and the design may seem dull or uninteresting. Similarly, if elements are almost, but not exactly, the same size, a viewer might not notice the differences in scale, and the hierarchy will be obscured. When using scale it is generally better to clearly differentiate the size of objects.

PROBLEMS WITH DIGITAL SCALING

The scale of visual elements can be altered in most computer software applications. Unfortunately, the ease with which you can change an object's size sometimes results in distortions of type or imagery. Whenever possible, you should maintain the proportions of an original image or piece of type. Distorted type is difficult to read, and images that have been made too large or too small can cause confusion for the viewer. Holding down the shift key when manually changing the size of an object will maintain constrained proportions in most software programs. If using a drop-down or flyaway menu (see below) to scale, make sure the box labeled "constrained proportions" is chosen. Always double check scaled objects. If they appear lopsided or squished, then the proportions weren't constrained and you should go back to the original file/version and rescale. Scaling is also important when considering appropriate resolution for both print and screen-based designs. If the resolution is too low, images can break down and appear pixelated both on screen and in print. Too high a resolution is also problematic when working on screen-based designs. Images larger than 72 dpi can require longer load times. For more information on how scaling affects production of images for print production, see page 214.

SCALE

In design, the term "scale" is often used as a verb and refers to changing the size of an object. For instance, in a critique, one might be told to scale up (enlarge) or down (reduce) an image or headline.

DROP-DOWN

Drop-down or flyaway menus exist in most design software. They are not seen until the user clicks on them, and then they offer secondary options for changing the attributes of an element or file. Once the user has made his/her choice, they revert back to the inactive state.

Original

Enlarged with proportions constrained

Enlarged without proportions constrained

above

Can you tell which image has been scaled without constraining proportions? Incorrectly scaling type is one of the marks of an inexperienced designer. If you need letterforms to be very close together consider using a condensed version of a font (see p. 119).

left

When working with physical space, scale becomes an important tool to draw viewers' attention and can also be used to differentiate rooms or areas within rooms. Notice how going over the support column with the large letters of the word London connects the glass panels and provides contrast against the large red wall at the back of the space.

Design: Kuhlmann Leavitt, St. Louis, Missouri

right

The large text is still readable because it was scaled proportionally. The scale of visual elements indicates hierarchy, and unless given other cues, viewers will read larger text first.

Design: Cheah Wei Chun, CLANHOUSE, Singapore

PROUDLY PRESENTED BY
MONT BLANC

Most Glam, isu yang selalu ditunggu-tunggu kembali dengan aura Grace Kelly berinspirasi era 50–an. Semua barang kemas dan jam tangan daripada Montblanc dan berbusana mewah Dior.

KONSEP & PENATA GAYA: CHEAH WEI CHUN,CLANHOUSEONLINE.COM. GAMBAR: BUSTANAM MOKHTAR/WHITE STUDIO. DANDANAN: OLIVIA OOI, DIBANTU OLEH ELENG. SOLEKAN: SHENG SAW@SHENGSAW.COM MENGGUNAKAN ESTEE LAUDER, DIBANTU OLEH JOYCE/ESTEE LAUDER & YEN YAP. PENYELARAS: AIZAT ABID, MISA'HALID & ATEENA SYUKRY. TEKS: JACKY HUSSEIN

PROXIMITY

Proximity refers to the relative distance between objects in space or time. Proximity can be used to produce emphasis in a variety of ways. When two very different types of visual material are placed next to each other, the contrast resulting from the pairing will create a focal point. On the other hand, the greater the distance between elements, the more they will stand out on their own. The isolation of an image or piece of text denotes importance because the negative space around it helps the viewer notice the form within it. Proximity is particularly useful at providing visual connections in motion graphics where imagery and other visual material can be arranged so individual elements are seen either together or in immediate succession. This allows viewers to quickly make associations and connect the visuals to the concept. When used as an organizing principle, proximity is most effective when the variation is noticeable and purposeful—for example, when several items are placed close together and others are given more space.

VISUAL TENSION

The term "visual tension" is used to describe instances where the placement of elements draws the eye to a particular area of a composition or when one side of a composition is too heavily weighted or has too much emphasis. Most often visual tension occurs when two or more elements are too close to each other or to a compositional edge. When this happens, the complexity of the shapes or space creates an unwanted focal point. Incorrect use of proximity is one of the most common causes of visual tension. When elements are placed too near each other there can be visual tension, but it also happens when the asymmetry of a composition is too extreme. It is usually best to put a noticeable amount of space between elements in a composition or to intentionally overlap them with each other or with the edge of the page. Since the interaction of form is always relative, there is no absolute measure for when items are too close. You should check a composition by evaluating whether any of the spaces between elements appears accidental or poorly considered. If elements nearly touch each other or the edge of the page, you should consider revising the placement. Overlapping is usually acceptable as long as it is intentional. There are times when visual tension can be positive. For example, the tension between elements might complement content, draw the eye through a composition, or provide a needed focal point.

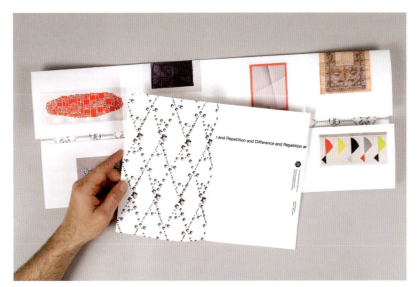

above

This piece shows how you can place images in proximity to each other while still giving each its own space. The repeated elements in the foreground help direct the viewer's eye to the left where text is placed.

Design: Project Projects, New York

right

The following example highlights an instance when proximity has been used incorrectly, thereby producing visual tension.

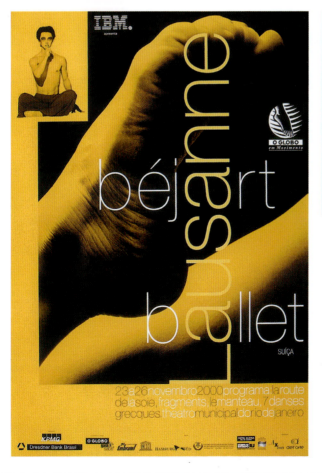

CONTRAST

Contrast is essentially difference. The greater the difference between two things, the greater the contrast will be. Effective use of contrast is one of the best ways to differentiate elements and activate negative space. Contrast may be achieved in a variety of ways. For example you can modify the value (see Chapter 4: Working with Color), or you can juxtapose any two dissimilar elements or visual material with different attributes. Placing large shapes or type next to much smaller elements provides contrast, as will two images with contradictory content or meaning. Figure-ground relationships (see p. 70) are one of the most basic forms of contrast. Any time an element is placed on a different color ground the distinction will be noticeable. The degree of variance in hues and values or in scale will determine which element stands out the most. Too little contrast and the composition will be static and boring. Too many instances of intense contrast and the hierarchy will be obscured and the viewer might be confused about where to look.

above

Because the letterforms are so large and are geometric, they are able to bleed off the edge of the page without having any small shapes at the edge that could create visual tension.

Design: Rebecca Foster Design, Birmingham, United Kingdom

left

Contrast can be achieved with color, with shape, and with scale. This poster uses all three variables and maximizes the contrast between the image and the yellow background.

Design: Felipe Taborda, Rio de Janeiro, Brazil

above

Contrast and shape make these matchbooks advertising an electrician's services stand out. When you are trying to use contrast in your own work, consider limiting yourself to one or two colors.

Design: Afterhours, Kent, United Kingdom

VISUAL WEIGHT

Each element in a layout has a degree of emphasis, and this relative importance is called visual weight. Like scale, emphasis and weight are related to hierarchy (see p. 72). When elements are more noticeable they are considered to be dominant. When they are less noticeable they are subordinate. Big shapes and bright colors stand out more than small objects, and they have greater visual weight than elements whose value is subdued. When evaluating visual weight consider where the eye focuses first, second, and third. Then assess why those objects or areas of the composition command attention and what could be done to change the current ordering. How a viewer's eye travels around a space or composition will determine understanding because the reading of a design is based on visual emphasis.

above

Each item in a composition has a particular visual weight. In this piece, the circles have the greatest visual weight because of their size and color. Keep in mind that both scale and color can be used to achieve greater visual weight.

Design: Anagrama, Nuevo Leon, Mexic

above

The visual weight of the letters HOP provide emphasis, and the contrast between the yellow and the black makes the text stand out and instantly tells the viewer which text to read first. You can try using contrast or weight (see p. 79) to make text stand out against the background.

Design: &Larry, Singapore

EMPHASIS

Common ways of creating emphasis
(or showing hierarchy, p. 72)

Value

Hue

Contrast

Scale

Variation or repetition

Proximity

FORM AND MEANING

Seeing is a combination of the physical act of processing visuals and the brain's interpretation of images based on literal meaning, memory, and contextual associations. Formal elements and images have both literal and associated meaning. A variety of interpretations can be attributed to an image showing a child and a car, but once text is added it will easily communicate a message about teenage drivers and insurance. When viewers engage in a decoding of messages, they will evaluate all the elements of a design and derive meaning. It is the designer's job to ensure that the content of a message and the form are complementary and enhance, rather than interfere with, correct decoding of messages. Design decisions should always be made for a reason and be rooted in meaning, audience considerations, and the external context where the final output will be seen or used. Avoid producing work dominated by style or decoration. It may initially seem trendy but will have no staying power. A sensitive designer will create original solutions that use expression and experimentation at the same time as effectively conveying the message.

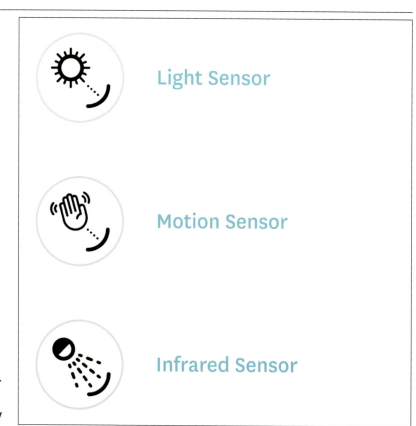

Light Sensor

Motion Sensor

Infrared Sensor

above

This example shows how simple forms can be used to express complicated ideas or actions. The viewer's previous associations with the images will make each icon easier to understand. Notice how they are all rendered in a similar way. Harmony of form and message is particularly important when designing a set of icons that may be seen without the presence of text.

Design: Cast Iron Design, Boulder, Colorado

left

Images of spices, vegetables and fruit are used to help promote this cleansing drink on social media.

Design: Afterhours, Kent, United Kingdom

LESS IS MORE

Design is a combination of structure and freedom. Complex projects begin with analytical activities like reading, research, and analysis (see Chapter 2) and then move to visual exploration and eventually to production and dissemination. It can be tempting to fill a space with form to make a composition look more designed. Over the top, form-filled layouts can be successful, but it is usually best to begin learning about design by using form sparingly. Try to use the fewest elements possible to convey a message. During the experimentation phase of a project it can be difficult to decide which elements to include and which to exclude, but with practice and feedback from peers and instructors you can develop a sense of how much visual material is needed to meet the objectives of a project or design brief.

The Portland Hospital
for Women & Children

above

It can be tempting to fill up all the space in a composition, but doing so often obstructs hierarchy. This brochure cleverly matches form and meaning and leaves large areas of the page open. The negative space makes the viewer focus on the various elements on the page. You can do the same thing by incorporating large amounts of white space in some of your projects.

Design: Rebecca Foster Design, Birmingham, United Kingdom

CHAPTER IN REVIEW:
Do's and don'ts

1. Activate and consider the entire compositional space. Avoid clustering visuals in the middle of the page. Include cropping or bleeding elements off the page/edge if appropriate. (p. 76)

2. Pay equal attention to positive and negative space and avoid creating cluttered layouts unless visual elements are purposely used as texture. (pp. 69 and 71)

3. Consider working with simple abstract forms (such as lines, points, and shapes) to communicate concepts and ideas or use these elements for organizational purposes. (pp. 64–66)

4. Connect form and meaning (this concept is discussed in more detail in Chapter 2). (p. 81)

5. Strive for visual rather than absolute balance. (p. 72)

6. Use scale to show the relative importance of elements in a composition and maintain proportions of shape, type, and image when scaling. (pp. 72 and 74)

7. Avoid instances of where negative visual tension disrupts or distracts from the overall composition. (p. 78)

8. Experiment with variables such as scale, proximity, contrast, and placement to alter how form behaves in a composition. (p. 80)

9. Evaluate content and test different arrangements of elements on the page to find the most dynamic arrangement while striving for harmony of the visual form and the message or content. (p. 81)

Chapter 4 / Working with Color

CHAPTER 4:
Working with Color

KEY TERMS AND CONCEPTS:

Additive color closely mimics how light stimulates the eye, and this system is used in screen design. (p. 88)

Brightness refers to the relative degree of lightness or darkness of a color. (p. 89)

Color is perceived by the eye when light reflects off different surfaces. The length and quality of the light being reflected produces a variety of types and intensity of color. (p. 86)

Color palette is a limited set of colors that have been chosen for use in composition or set of design deliverables. Color palettes often include dominant tones, which are used frequently or for more important content, as well as subordinate or accent colors, which are used more sparingly. (p. 88)

Color theory refers to practical analysis of how hues relate to each other and what happens when two or more hues are mixed in different proportions. (p. 99)

Cool colors have underlying tones of blue. (p. 96)

Complementary colors occur at opposite points on the color wheel, and when combined they produce a neutral like brown, gray, or black. When placed next to each other they have a high degree of contrast and may seem to visually vibrate off each other. Examples of complementary colors include red and green and blue and orange. (p. 92)

Hue is another term for color. The two words are used interchangeably. (p. 89)

Monotones (or monochromatic) are color schemes produced using a single color plus its tints and shades. (p. 94)

Neutrals are colors including black, white, gray, and muted tones of brown or beige. (p. 95)

Saturation (also called chroma) is the intensity, strength, or purity of a color without the addition of black or white. (p. 89)

Shade is the variation of a color plus black. (p. 89)

Subtractive color is a model based on the primary colors red, blue, and yellow, and it mimics the spectrum of colors used by artists. (p. 88)

Temperature is the perceived warmth or coolness of a color. (p. 89)

Tint is the variation of a color plus white. (p. 89)

Value is the relative degree of lightness or darkness of a color. Adding white or black will change the value of a color. (p. 95)

Warm colors are hues with underlying tones of red. (p. 96)

WHAT IS COLOR?

What comes to mind when you think about color? Is it the green of a leaf, the red of a sports car, or the color of your favorite shirt? Color is all around us, and even though it feels "real" and concrete, color is actually produced by varying wavelengths of light. When light is reflected off a surface, the human eye perceives those wavelengths and we recognize color. The specific hue our eye sees is determined by the degree to which a surface can first reflect light and then produce waves of different lengths. Since light is the route of all colors, individual hues and value will be affected by ambient light in a room and by the intensity of pigments used to generate various shades and tints.

White might appear to be the absence of color, but it isn't. White contains all colors, and the absence of color produces black. This can be confusing because combining multiple pigments produces black when you work with ink or paint. The resulting mixture reflects so little light that black is perceived. In print projects and artwork, inks and paint are mixed to produce surfaces with varied degrees of reflectiveness. On computer or tablet screens, color is produced when light of varying intensity is emitted from each quadrant of the display.

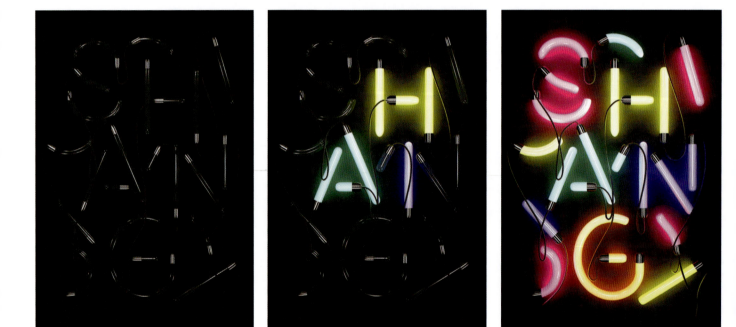

above

Design: Goetz Gramlich,
Heidelberg, Germany

SUBJECTIVE ASSOCIATIVE MEANING

People feel color as much as they see it. Color symbolizes ideas and evokes meaning. The connotations linked to colors are subjective and will always be influenced by place, age, gender, personal experience, religion, and ethnicity of the viewer. In Europe and the Americas brides wear white, but in Asian countries brides tend to wear brighter, more intense colors, and red plays an important role in traditional Chinese bridal ceremonies where it signifies happiness. White is associated with funerals in some countries, whereas dark colors like blacks or grays indicate mourning in others. As you identify hues to be used in a particular project, it is important to be sensitive to any cultural connotations affecting a viewer's perception of the design. What works in New York might not have the same meaning in Bangkok or Mexico City.

WHAT WE SEE

The *visible spectrum* refers to a limited range of colors distinguishable by the human eye. These hues include red, orange, yellow, green, blue, blue violet, and violet. When further limited to the colors that are most distinct from each other, we have what are called primary colors. Red, green, and blue are the primary colors in the visible spectrum. In total, the human eye can discern approximately 10 million colors, all of which come from a combination of these basic primary colors.

left

Look at how color changes this composition. Blue is typically associated with boys and pink with girls; by changing the color from blue to pink the designer challenges the viewer's previous associations with color and creates a gender neutral palette.

Design: Cheah Wei Chun, CLANHOUSE, Singapore

right

These variations show how changing color can alter a viewer's perception of an image. Notice how blue, a primary color, is used twice, but the design appears quite different depending on whether bright or dark blue is used. Try changing one or more colors in a design to see how different hues alter hierarchy.

Design: Genevieve Hitchings, New York

COLOR WHEEL DIAGRAMS

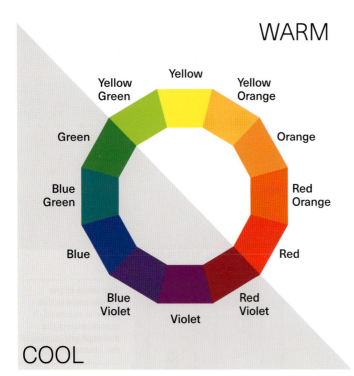

WARM

Yellow
Green

Yellow

Yellow
Orange

Green

Orange

Blue
Green

Red
Orange

Blue

Red

Blue
Violet

Red
Violet

Violet

COOL

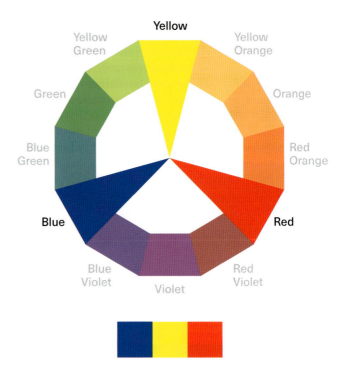

Yellow
Green

Yellow

Yellow
Orange

Green

Orange

Blue
Green

Red
Orange

Blue

Red

Blue
Violet

Red
Violet

Violet

Basic color wheel
with warm and cool temperatures indicated

Primary hues
Primary colors include red, yellow, and blue. They are pure hues, which are unrelated to each other. By mixing primary colors with each other, it is possible to create any color in the spectrum.

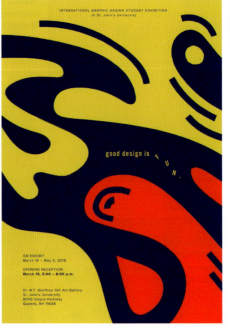

left

Primary colors can form the basis for bright, eye-catching color palette.

Design: Jessica Monteavaro Garbin, New York

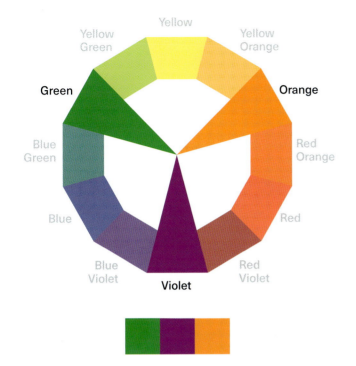

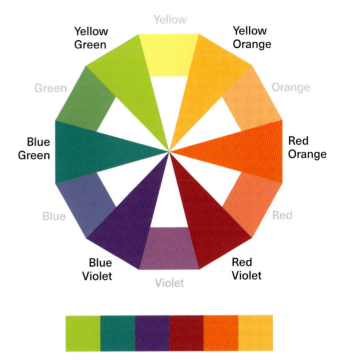

Secondary hues

Secondary colors include orange, green, and violet. They are produced when equal amounts of primary colors are combined.

Tertiary hues

Tertiary colors are located between primary and secondary hues on the color wheel and have more of one primary color than the other. The appearance of a tertiary color will depend on which primary color is dominant in the mixture.

left

The color palette used in this composition is based on secondary colors. This color combination is a bit unexpected but is a good match for the term "exciting."

Design: Maria Torres, New York

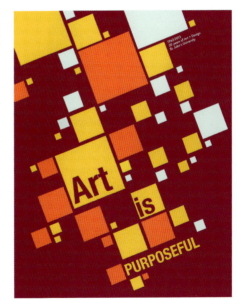

left

A warm, dark red is the dominant primary in this tertiary combination. If you exchanged the warm, red background color for blue or yellow, the composition would appear quite different.

Design: Taylor Slyder, New York

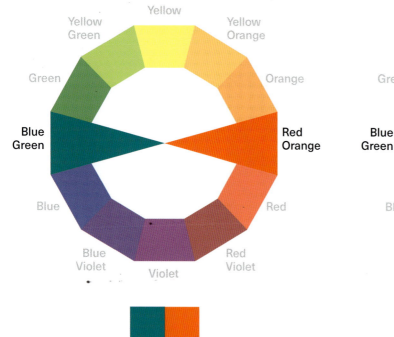

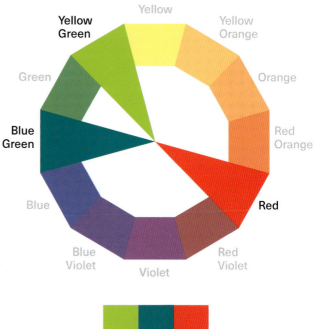

Complementary hues

Complementary hues are opposite from each other on the color wheel and have the greatest degree of contrast. When combined, complimentary colors cancel each other out and create a neutral tone.

Split complements

Split complementary hues refer to a group of hues including a primary color and two secondary colors that are located adjacent the hues' complement on the color wheel.

left

___

This design primarily uses the complementary colors yellow and blue. A bit of red/orange was added to balance the composition. Complementary colors can seem loud and garish when placed next to each other, so be careful not to use these color combinations in situations where the message of the text conflicts with the color palette.

Design: Artiana Wynder, New York

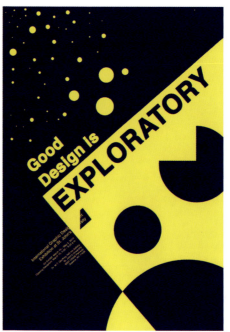

left

___

This composition uses the principles of split complementary colors but includes only blue/violet and yellow rather than also using red/violet in the color palette.

Design: Steven Verdile, New York

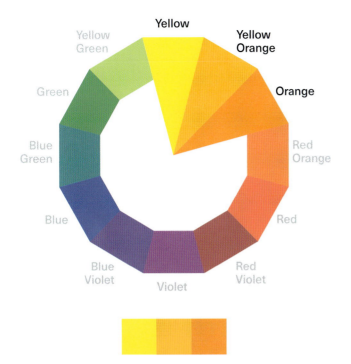

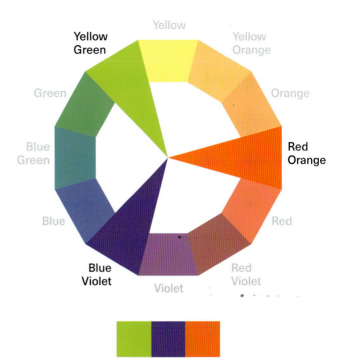

Analogous harmonies

Analogous combinations are a group of hues including a primary hue and two adjacent hues next to each other on the color wheel. Analogous color combinations tend to be harmonious because they reflect similar wavelengths of light.

Triad harmonies

Triad harmonies are groups where any three hues are spaced at equal distances from each other around the color wheel. Because primary and secondary colors are equidistant from each other, they combine to create a triadic color combination.

left

This poster show uses an analogous color combination. By adding the gradient, the designer shows the transition in tones and draws the eye down from the top to the bottom of the composition.

Design: Jessica Monteavaro Garbin, New York

left

This composition uses a palette based on triadic harmonies. Since we don't often think about these color combinations, it is often best to start by using an online color picker when developing triadic harmonies.

Design: Liz Marcotte, New York

Tetrad harmonies

Tetrad combinations are made up of four complementary or split complementary hues.

Monochromatic hue

Monochromatic colors are variations of a single hue including tints (the hue plus white) and shades (the hue plus black). Like analogous colors, monochromatic color combinations are considered to be harmonious.

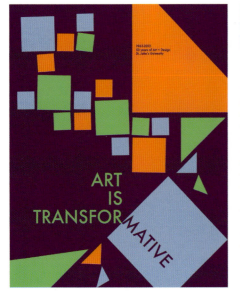

left
___

The color palette used in this composition uses a tetrad combination. By using some colors as the dominant and others as subordinate, one can use all four colors together in a single design without creating confusion.

Design: Taylor Slyder, New York

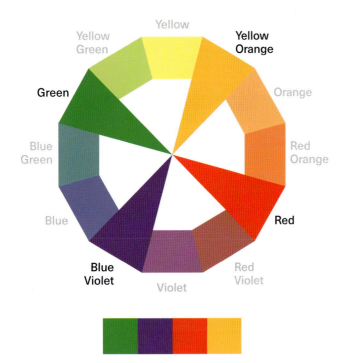

left
___

Monochromatic compositions don't have to be boring. By picking a bright color and then using its shades, one can increase the visual interest of a composition. Monochromatic combinations are also less expensive to produce if you are sending a design to an offset (see p. 212) printer.

Design: Veronica Farias, New York

NEUTRAL COLORS

Neutral colors include black, white, gray, and muted tones of brown or beige. These hues don't show up on the color wheel, and they are often overlooked when one makes initial decisions about color. Neutrals can be used on their own or they can be added to a more complex color palette. Like other colors, neutral tones can be distinguished by whether they are warm or cool. If you have ever had to buy house paint, you have probably seen how many different variations of neutral colors can exist. A company might produce ten or more versions of white. Each "white" will be distinguished by its brightness and whether it is cool or warm. Like paint, the paper used to print design projects comes in a variety of shades of white. How pigmented ink appears on the surface of paper will change depending on how bright the paper is and whether it has underlying cool or warm tones. On their own, neutral colors are often associated with softer subjects like spas, household items, furniture, and hotels, but there are also examples of neutral colors being used for edgier subjects. Since they rarely have direct associations, neutral tones are very versatile, and they can be either masculine or feminine.

VALUE

Value is the relative lightness or darkness of a color. On its own, hue is stronger than value. For example, gray tones blend together when used on a series of shapes, but add color to one of those shapes and it will stand out. Value can be used to achieve contrast. The greater the difference in value, the more contrast will occur. It is possible to create contrast without value using texture or other variables, but value does not exist without contrast. Value is also used to show relative importance/hierarchy (see p. 72). Two shapes with equal size and value will have the same importance, but change the value of one shape and it becomes dominant or subordinate. Altering the value of different elements in a composition is one way to indicate where a viewer should look first, second, and third. In other words, hierarchy can be indicated by making some elements darker and others lighter. Value is always affected by the external environment in which a hue is seen. When there is less light in a room, colors seem darker. But outdoors on a sunny day or under intense indoor lights, color and value will appear to be lighter/brighter.

below

The colors used in the image of the paint tube have a similar value to the background of this piece. Shifting the value of the shadow of the tube provides a bit of drama and makes the illustration stand out even though it is created using similar colors as the background.

Design: Stephan Bundi, Boll, Switzerland

left

A neutral color palette is used for the design of this mailer. Warm white and metallic brown create a combination that feels simple yet sophisticated.

Design: Sagenvier Design Kommunikation, Dornbin, Austria

left

This identity and stationery use neutral tones. The palette works well on its own but it is also great for pairing with imagery that might include brighter colors.

Design: Goetz Gramlich, Heidelberg, Germany

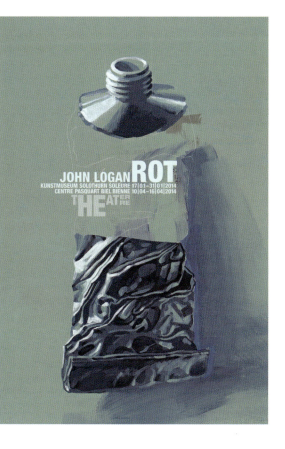

BRIGHT COLORS

Bright colors are made using pure pigment or are produced without the addition of black or white. Unnatural colors like fluorescents are also bright. Since they stand out, bright colors are a great tool to get a viewer's attention or to draw the eye to a particular part of a composition. Be careful not to use too many saturated or super-bright colors together in the same compositional space. These supercharged combinations can be irritating to the eye and interfere with hierarchy. Successful compositions sometimes rely on bright colors, but it is usually best to use another color like black or brown to offset an overly bright palette.

above

Bright colors and patterns help the viewer relate to the product produced by this bakery and candy store. The same bright palette is used for the company's identity and other collateral.

Design: Anagrama, Nuevo Leon, Mexico

right

A person who suffers from colorblindness might misinterpret the reference used here because he/she might not accurately see the color red in the illustration of the flag.

Design Studio Beuro, East Sussex, United Kingdom

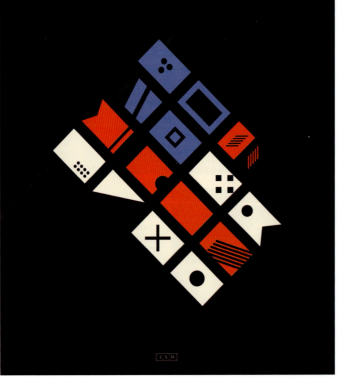

COLOR BLINDNESS

Humans perceive about 10 million distinctive colors, but not everyone has the same ability to differentiate between different colors. Color blindness is the inability to see certain colors. The condition occurs most often in men and affects approximately 8 percent of the population. Red-green color blindness is the most common. These men are unable to distinguish between red and green, and the resulting handicap may be a mere annoyance, but it can also have important ramifications depending on a person's career and the degree to which he is unable to tell red and green apart.

COLOR THEORY

Classification systems for color were introduced earlier in this chapter. They demonstrated the relationships between different hues on color wheel diagrams. Now we will learn about color theory, how these systems apply to real-world situations, and how they can be used in your design projects. Color theory refers to practical analysis of how hues relate to one another and what happens when two or more hues are mixed in different proportions. The basic tenets of color theory suggest that different color pairings produce a variety of visual effects, depending on how they are used.

Color theory helps us understand the real-world effects of color on objects and the environment while also providing guidance for how different pairings and combinations will change a viewer's perception of individual colors. In order to understand how hues and values relate to each other and how they operate within a composition, artists and designers use visual tools like color wheels (see p. 88) to map different groupings and their relational impact on other hues. Learning about color theory and distinctive categories of color will allow you to identify effective pairings more quickly.

When a color combination is pleasing it is considered to be in harmony or to be balanced. As we learned in the last chapter, we usually try to achieve visual rather than absolute balance. Since balance is always relative, what is considered balanced in one composition might be disruptive or simply neutral in another. When working with color, success is determined by whether a specific color choice has enhanced the message, whether it correctly targets the audience, and if it is optimal for the viewing context or environment.

One of the most useful principles of color theory suggests that the eye is always trying to achieve equilibrium. Research has shown that we tend to find pairings where the colors combine to produce a neutral more pleasing. This phenomenon is based on the idea of an afterimage. If you stare at a block of color and then look away you will see the complement of that color. The reason our brains produce this afterimage isn't fully understood, but it may have to do with the receptors in our eyes becoming fatigued and then producing a complement in the same value and intensity as the original hue. The implication is that our eyes and brain look for the balance or symmetry that comes by combining a hue with its opposite. You can use this principle to your advantage by including

left

Vivid colors like the ones used on this record cover demand attention and can form the basis for a design. Imagery is not needed because the transition between colors used on the album creates an engaging layout.

Design Studio Beuro, East Sussex, United Kingdom

TEACHING COLOR THEORY

Johannes Itten, a *master* instructor at the Bauhaus in Weimar, Germany, in the 1920s, is one of the greatest teachers of color theory ever to have lived. He outlined his ideas in *The Elements of Color* and detailed three ways to achieve successful color solutions. The first way is visually (he called this impression), the second is emotionally (which he called expression), and the third is symbolically (he called this construction). While Itten acknowledged that some color relationships have predictable outcomes, he believed that much of the way artists and designers use color, and audiences appreciate color, is subjective and determined by context. He therefore advised designers and artists to study the relationships hues have to each other in different situations as a means of improving color sensitivity and arriving at more meaningful color pairings.

Joseph Albers was a student of Itten's at the Bauhaus, where he taught after he graduated. A successful painter, Albers spent his life working with color in painting and design. After the Nazis closed the Bauhaus in 1933, Albers came to the United States, where he taught at Black Mountain College and Yale University. He spent years studying color and its effects on his students, and in 1963 he published the influential book *Interactions of Color*. Albers looked at how colors interact and what happens when hues are placed next to each other in the same composition. He used exercises to help his students create effective groupings. Like Itten, Albers believed a person's understanding of color was subjective and said that if you asked fifty students what they saw when they saw red, you would come back with fifty different shades of red. Both Itten and Albers believed that a person's ability to identify successful color pairings could be improved by practice and study.

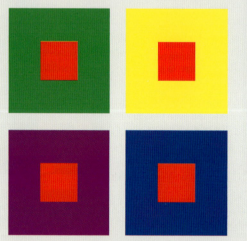

above

Itten's color wheel was designed to show the interaction between colors, and he believed we should approach color visually, emotionally, and symbolically. Unlike other color wheels, the primary colors are in the middle here, and the hues derived from mixing them are on the outside.

above

This example highlights the visual interaction that occurs when a color is placed on backgrounds of a different hue. This is a good example of how our perception of a hue changes depending on what other colors it is next to. When the red square is placed on the green, it creates the ghosting effect previously discussed. Notice how the red square seems to stand out on the blue and yellow background but recedes against the purple background.

above

Albers created numerous studies to show the relationship between different hues. This study shows two small squares of the same color in the center of each composition surrounded by different colors. Because of their proximity to different hues, the color of the squares appears to be different even though it is not. This example illustrates how a viewer's perception of color is always relative and is based on what other hues are next to it or are present in a composition.

EXERCISE:
Color compositions based on Itten's contrasts
Courtesy of Annette Cords

Create three compositions showing the different types of contrast outlined on the right side of this page. The assignment can be completed digitally using a program such as Adobe Illustrator or by hand with Color-aid paper. All compositions should be 6 × 6 inches.

1. Contrast of warm and cool

Select two warm colors and two cool colors. All colors should be similar to each other in value. Create a geometric or organic composition using shapes and lines. Then fill in areas of the composition so all colors touch at some point.

2. Simultaneous contrast

Find two colors that visually vibrate when you place them next to each other. Avoid choosing a straightforward complementary pair of colors. Create a composition that enhances this vibrating effect.

3. Contrast of extension or proportion

Select three colors with different degrees of brightness and saturation. You'll notice that some colors have more weight than others. Create a balanced composition by assigning proportional sizes to the visual weight of each color. Lighter and brighter colors have more weight and therefore need to occupy less space.

Digital production: Part 1) Save each composition on a separate art board or document. Part 2) Pick your most successful composition and apply the principles of warm and cool, simultaneous contrast and contrast of extension to that composition. Then use Adobe Photoshop to create an animated GIF showing how a single composition changes when different color pairings are applied.

Color-aid paper production: If using Color-aid paper, you should draw the shapes you intend to cut out on the back of the paper. This way you will avoid dirtying the colors with pencil lines. Use rubber cement or another adhesive (see Chapter 8) to mount your compositions on heavy weight paper. You should have a 2 inch border on all sides.

CHOOSING A COLOR PALETTE

Choosing a color palette requires a mixture of analysis, understanding basic principles of color theory, trial and error, and personal preference. For some projects it will be appropriate to create a palette using several different hues, but in other situations a limited color palette will be more successful. After you have identified specific hues for use in a color palette, further variations can be achieved by mixing a fully saturated hue with white (to achieve tints) or with black (to produce shades). Two separate colors can also be combined to produce a completely new color. Designers often excel when working within specified constraints, so consider limiting the number of colors you will work with before you begin a project.

Starting a design in black and white can be a good way to work on a project where color choice seems overwhelming. Using this system you can make initial decisions about placement and hierarchy without the distraction of color. After a rough draft has been developed, you can add in one or two colors at a time and experiment by applying different colors to each element in the design. The analogous or complementary pairings found on the color wheel diagrams are examples of well-known combinations that can easily be applied to design projects.

above

The design for this wine label uses only black and white. Depending on the physical context where they will be seen, simple one- or two-color palettes can stand out even more than color palettes with multiple hues.

Design: Anagrama, Nuevo Leon, Mexico

right

Red and green are used as a two-color combination for these tomato sauce labels. The color palette creates a good tie-in to what people already know about the product, and the use of different shades and tints allows for greater flexibility when creating the accompanying illustrations of tomatoes.

Design: Metalli Lindberg, Treviso, Italy

STEP-BY-STEP GUIDE TO WORKING WITH COLOR

The following steps can be used to create a color palette for use in design projects. Begin by completing steps 1 and 2 and then try some of the techniques listed to further develop the palette and to match it to the content and other elements in the project.

1. Identify why color is being used and what color choices should convey.

2. Create a palette using a combination of dominant, subordinate, and accent colors.

Techniques for experimentation

Once a particular hue is identified, try lighter or darker versions of the color to see what value works best. Limit the number of colors used in a composition. If other elements like photos or illustrations are used, consider sampling one or more colors from what already exists in the photos.

Finally, test several colors or color palettes in the layout to identify which is most successful.

WORKING WITH COLOR IN DESIGN SOFTWARE

Design students usually choose colors using the built-in color pickers in design software programs. These systems include an infinite number of colors, and with so many options, picking the best colors for a project can be difficult. Adobe Kuler, Pantone swatch books, and Paletton's Color Scheme Designer can be helpful when you need to identify effective color combinations. More robust online/onscreen tools like Kuler and Color Scheme Designer allow users to stipulate the number of colors they want to use and then to choose one of the groupings found on color wheel diagrams. The programs produce a number of variations based on those parameters. Other color matching/picking tools like swatch books simply show individual colors along with their tints and shades. Online tools and swatch books don't guarantee good color results, but they do quickly identify different pairings and can be a useful tool when you need to develop custom color palettes.

Online tools
Adobe Kuler: https://color.adobe.com

Adobe Capture: Is a free app that uses your photos to create color palettes. It is available for both iPhones and Android.

Color Scheme Designer: http://paletton.com

above

Working with online tools like Adobe Kuler or swatch books can help you get more comfortable making color choices.

DOMINANT/SUBORDINATE SYSTEM

The dominant/subordinate system (see example below) allows you to identify a three-color palette to be used in design projects. This method is particularly useful because it designates which hues will have more or less importance. Start by choosing a dominant color, either because you think it will complement the message (or content) being communicated or because it will appeal to the target audience. Then choose a subordinate hue to complement or contrast with the initial color. It can be helpful to use a color wheel to help choose the second color. Next you should identify an accent color. As the name suggests, accents are used less frequently than dominant and subordinate colors. Accents can be a tint or shade of one of the dominant or subordinate colors, a neutral tone, or a completely new color. Experimentation is key. Try to replace the subordinate color with another hue to see if the overall combination is more pleasing. Alter the saturation of one or more colors and see if it improves the overall effect of the color pairings. Finally, test the colors from several combinations in a layout to see which enhances the message and the content.

COLOR SELECTION

- Pick dominant, subordinate, and accent colors.

- Explore variations including tints and shades.

- Try replacing one color with its complement and assess whether the new pairing is more harmonious.

- Experiment with limited color palettes.

- Explore neutrals as well as more fully saturated hues.

Dominant Subordinate Accent

above

The dominant color used in this identity is a brown tone reminiscent of the color of wood. A lighter tan is subordinate. Changing one color from dominant to subordinate will alter your layout and give it a very different appearance.

Design: This is Folly, Minneapolis, Minnesota

ONE-COLOR PALETTES

Professional designers usually choose to work with limited color palettes because printing fewer colors is less expensive, but monochromatic and black and white combinations are also a good choice for student projects. The fewer colors in play, the easier it will be to develop and maintain visual hierarchy. Similarly, black and white offer optimum contrast and are a good choice when you want your designs to stand out or when they will be seen in a busy visual environment.

When developing a monochromatic palette it is usually best to begin by identifying a single hue. Bright or saturated hues tend to work best. You can either use a single color by itself or use the color along with black. You can also add one or more tints and shades of the dominant color as long as they have the same base and are distinctive. In a one-color palette, the color can be used in the ground/background or it can be applied to elements in the composition. Remember, when working with text, contrast is key. If you are going to use a single color, you should choose a hue that will contrast against the background and other visual elements.

PRINTING BLACK

There are two ways of producing the color black when you are printing on paper. In the first scenario, black is produced by moving the slider all the way to "k" (or key). This system is used for one-color jobs and for black text. However, when there are large areas of black in a composition, the white of the paper often shows through the black ink, producing a mottled, unsaturated appearance. To achieve a rich black, you can create a new swatch using 60 percent cyan, 60 percent magenta, 40 percent yellow, and 100 percent black or "key." This combination of pigments produces a rich black that is pleasing to the eye and effectively covers the white or the ground or paper. Files should always use the CMYK mode regardless of which method you use. If a project requires both types of black, it is helpful to create a separate swatch for each.

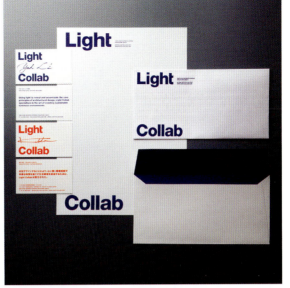

left

One-color palettes can provide contrast against the background, and in this case color indicates hierarchy and the viewer clearly knows which information is most important. Collateral such as business cards and letterhead often only use one color. If you are doing a project like this, choose a color that complements some aspect of the company you are working for.

Design: &Larry, Singapore

left

Bright orange is used as the dominant color for this exhibition design. Artifacts and images provide secondary colors. Light draws the viewer's attention to certain areas of the space and should be considered another visual element when you are designing spaces.

Design: Project Projects, New York

left

The design for these beer labels uses illustration rather than color as the primary tool to communicate content. On a crowded shelf, this one-color palette can stand out even more than bottles designed in full color.

Design: Eduardo Bertone, Madrid, Spain

TWO-COLOR PAIRINGS

Two color pairings are a good choice when you want to work with a simple palette but still need some degree of color variation in a project. Using pre-established pairings such as those outlined on the color wheels can provide a basis for color selection, but you can also choose unusual or offbeat color combinations. When working with two colors it is helpful to identify one color as dominant and the other as subordinate. There are times when both hues can play an equal role in the composition, but to avoid creating static, one-dimensional compositions, these pairings should be complemented by other variables like contrast and scale. Two-color palettes include colors plus the white of the paper or screen. If you intend to print on a colored paper or other material, then you need to plan your color palette accordingly. Not all colors show up well on a non-white background.

CUSTOM COLORS

Using custom colors almost always works better than the default swatches found in software programs. Once you have identified several colors using a color picker, create a custom swatch of each. Test more and less intense versions of the same color in the layout. If colors seem to vibrate against each other, try reducing the value or choosing less saturated colors.

right

Both versions of this piece use pink plus one other color and black. Notice the difference between the version with blue and the one with yellow. These posters are two of a pair; however, you can try creating similar variations as tests when you are working on school projects.

Design: Aufuldish & Warinner, San Anselmo, California

IMAGE-BASED COLOR PALETTES

The tones present within an image (photograph or fine art) can form the basis for the color palette used in an entire composition. This system requires you to sample existing colors in an image and will provide visual connections between photographic and illustrative material and the rest of the design. Start by identifying the different tones present in the photo. Then sample several colors using the eyedropper in a software application like Adobe Photoshop. Create small swatches of the sampled colors on your Artboard and decide which will be dominant and subordinate. Experiment by applying the tones to other elements in the composition and even to the background. Test several variations using different combinations of colors applied to the visual elements. A composition will appear more unified if you repeat the tints and shades several times within the same layout.

left

Color will affect how an image is perceived by the viewer. Notice the difference between the images. When neutral tones are used, the image doesn't carry as much specific meaning. Similarly, when there isn't enough contrast between the background and the shapes in the foreground, the visual has less prominence and seems to be somewhat obscured. In the bottom example there is optimum contrast, and the red color extends the meaning of the image and gives the skull a creepy look.

right

When you are working with images, you can pick up one of the colors in the image for use in a color palette. Here, the purplish color in the background of the photograph creates a visual tie-in to the interior of the design.

Design: This is Folly, Minneapolis, Minnesota

COLOR REPETITION

Repeating one or more hues in a composition is an excellent way to use color to develop dynamic visual space. This system can be used to create unity or to visually connect two or more elements. Repetition usually works best when the color palette is limited and/or when one limits how many colors a viewer sees at once (e.g., one page or screen at a time). If too many different colors are repeated, a composition will appear to be disorganized and hierarchy may be obscured. Repetition of one or more colors also gives continuity to layouts. For example, using the same color for two pieces of text on the same page tells the viewer the elements have some connection. The same technique can also help lead the viewer's eye around a page or screen. When viewers see the same color on several pages, they will naturally connect the content. Repetition of colors provides flow and can enhance the visual relationship between pages or different deliverables in a campaign.

COLOR AND HIERARCHY

When used well, color can enhance a viewer's understanding of content. But because it is such a strong visual signifier, it can also disrupt the intended hierarchy (for an in-depth discussion of hierarchy as it relates to typography see p. 122). Small amounts of a bright or very light color can override other variables such as size. Brightly colored small shapes may even appear larger than objects with greater physical size if those objects have a more muted tone. In general, the colors you choose should support visual hierarchy and help viewers understand where to look at first, second, and third. As you evaluate whether the colors in the composition are successful, it is important to assess how each element reacts with the others. Remember, bright, white, or intense colors will stand out, whereas dull, dark colors will recede. The color palette you choose for a project needs to accommodate all the visual elements and typographic expressions. If it does not do so effectively, it should be revised.

above

Repeating the same two colors connects these two advertisements even though the compositions are different. If you are designing a series of pieces, consider connecting them visually with color.

Design Eduardo Bertone, Madrid, Spain

right

Color adds interest to this book cover without disrupting the visual hierarchy. Remember, color can trump scale, so make sure hierarchy is maintained when using a bright color palette.

Design: Bruketa&Zinic, Zagreb, Croatia

CONTRAST AND COLOR

Even more than the color itself, contrast will determine whether elements such as type, shape, and image are visually distinct or blend together. As stated previously, if two or more colors are used together, it is usually best to show a noticeable difference in the tones. For example, yellow will immediately stand out against blue, but two tones of yellow with only a slight difference in value may blend together or look unintentional. The least legible combinations are red on blue, orange on blue, yellow on orange, and green on orange. In these pairings, the colors seem to vibrate against each other, creating visual tension. When you have a dark background, try using lighter or brighter colors on top. Do the reverse if the background is light. Contrast is very useful in design, but too much contrast can be irritating or may even cause confusion. Contrast should support the inherent hierarchy of the text.

left

The brightly colored foreground shapes contrast against the black and white imagery in these posters. Contrast is one of the best ways to make a viewer notice your work, so try using bright/light colors against a dark background or vice versa.

Design: Project Projects, New York

EXERCISE:
Evaluating color choices

Assessing whether the visual choices you made on a project were successful will help you identify what worked well and what could use improvement. Start by developing several iterations of a design with different color combinations using the guide on page 105. This process may seem tedious, but it will allow you to practice identifying which solutions most effectively communicate the message and/or engage the end user. As you become more confident, try experimenting with more challenging color palettes like those that contain heavily saturated tones or very bright colors. Once you have one or more layouts ready, use the following questions to evaluate the effectiveness of colors in the design.

1. **What was the intent of the color choices used in the project?**

2. **Does the color palette enhance the content or does it disrupt readability or visual hierarchy?**

3. **Did the colors help achieve the correct response to the design (i.e., do viewers want to buy the product or do they know where and how to attend an event)?**

4. **How could the color palette or use of color in the composition be improved?**

CHAPTER IN REVIEW:
Do's and don'ts

1. Evaluate the goals of a project before you start and connect color choice to the message being communicated, audience considerations, and the final context in which a design will be seen or used. (p. 99)

2. Keep in mind subjective meanings and ensure your audience won't have any unintended associations with the color used in the design. (p. 87)

3. Avoid using hues where the values are too closely related if colored objects or visuals in the design need to be distinct from each other. (p. 111)

4. Work with color wheels to help determine which hues will be more or less suited for the project. (p. 88)

5. Work in the correct color mode for the intended output (RGB = screen, CMYK = print). (p. 88)

6. Try limited color palettes to help create a sense of continuity. These systems are especially useful on multipage/screen documents and in series of outputs for a single organization or product. (p. 106)

7. Develop a color palette including dominant, accent, and subordinate hues (if applicable) before you begin to place elements in a layout. (p. 106)

8. Consider adding neutral tones to a color palette or creating a palette dominated by neutrals. (p. 95)

9. Make sure your use of color doesn't disrupt the hierarchy of the content. (p. 110)

10. Try purposely connecting or contrasting the color palette with the hues in images and/or other visual material. (p. 111)

11. Test several variations of your color palette on the content to analyze which one is most successful. (p. 111)

CHAPTER 5: Typography

KEY TERMS AND CONCEPTS:

Black (when used to describe a typeface) refers to a heavy-weight version of a typeface and is normally even heavier than bold. (p. 119)

Book weight (also see *Roman*) typefaces are designed for setting large amounts of text. They can be heavier, lighter, or the same weight as the roman or mid-weight version of the typeface. (see *weight* p. 119)

Condensed typefaces reduce the width of individual characters. Condensed, extra condensed, and compressed are all terms associated with different degrees of width. The opposite of a condensed typeface is one where the characters have been extended. (see Univers type family p. 119)

Body copy (also called body text or running text) refers to multiple lines of text set together and/or text that is set in paragraph format. (p. 125)

Italics and **obliques** are slanted versions of a typeface and are used to express emphasis. Unlike obliques, which are simply slanted, Italics are a different version of a typeface with certain letters designed specifically to appear correctly with the slant.

Dashes are used to punctuate breaks or pauses and connections between words or parts of sentences. Em dashes indicate a break in a thought and are used instead of colons or semicolons, where as an en dash is used instead of a hyphen and to indicate a connection between things or names. Em dashes are as wide as the letter M, and en dashes are as wide as a capital N. (p. 138)

Display type (also called display text) is larger type typically used for headlines or titles. Text type can also be used as

display if the letterforms are clearly visible when they are enlarged. Display type may require extra kerning to ensure letters appear evenly spaced. (p. 145)

Extended typefaces have wider characters than the medium or roman versions of the typeface.

Hyphenation is the marked syllabic division of words. (p. 137)

Kerning is the space between two characters of text. To achieve visually even spacing between letters, adjustment of kerning is often needed. (p. 130)

Light or lightweight typefaces have less weight than the roman or medium version of the typeface, and many typefaces typically exist on a continuum weight from ultra light or hair through ultra black. (see *weight* p. 119)

Orphan refers to instances where a word exists by itself on a line. Orphans should be avoided. To do so, use tracking or hyphenation to bring the word up onto the line before or to bring another word down onto the line with it. (p. 138)

Roman is a mid-weight version of a font. Typefaces with smaller families often include only roman, light, bold, and italic/oblique. (also see *book weight*)

Rule is another word for lines and is specifically used when describing lines in design compositions. (p. 136)

Sans serif typefaces do not have extra elements added to the strokes of the letterforms. (p. 117)

Serifs are small elements added to the terminal (p. 117) strokes of letterforms. Typefaces are classified by whether they have these elements. (p. 117)

Tracking is the space between the characters of text or words. (p. 131)

Type classification refers to the ways different typefaces are divided into categories and subcategories according to their appearance. Common ways for categorizing type include weight or stroke of characters and the way each part of a letter ends (also see *serif*). (p. 117)

Type family refers to the collection of different weights and iterations of a typeface. (see Univers type family p. 119)

Type foundries own the rights to the design of typefaces and will sell digital versions of a typeface to the general public. The cost of a typeface varies considerably based on who designed it and whether it comes with an extended family or not. (p. 143)

Typesetting is the visual arrangement of text. The term dates back to when individual letters of metal type were "set" together to form the compositional arrangements used in printing. Today, typesetting is primarily digital and refers to working with (or "setting") large amounts of text.

Typographer is someone who designs typefaces. He/she may be commissioned to design a typeface for a particular client or may initiate the design of a new typeface on his/her own. (p. 143)

Weight is the thickness or thinness of a typeface. (p. 119)

Widow is a single line of text in a column by itself. Widows should be avoided because they cause unnecessary breaks in the text. (p. 138)

WHAT IS TYPOGRAPHY?

Typography is the visual expression of the written word. Individual letters are animated and idiosyncratic. They come together to form alphabets, the all-important building blocks of language. When letters are combined they create words, sentences, paragraphs, and eventually entire stories. The most fundamental goal of typography is to communicate information. To be clear, typography works when it conveys a message regardless of whether the type is written with a magic marker, spelled out in dots and dashes, or styled using elegant letterforms.

Consider the flyers advertising student groups on campus. Do they look like they were created by a designer (see image example below)? Probably not. But you understand their meaning nonetheless. The flyers have met the minimum requirement for typography, but they are unlikely to be memorable. For design projects to be successful, you need to learn about the distinguishing characteristics of typefaces, how to align and arrange type for optimal viewing, and different ways of conveying emphasis using typographic forms. Graphic designers revel in the interplay between the pure form (shape) of type and the meaning it conveys. Quotation marks, commas, single words, captions, and lists can all be used as the raw material for layout and compositions. This chapter covers the most basic principles for distinguishing letterforms and arranging and styling type. Practice the fundamentals of good typography on every project. Little by little what initially seems counterintuitive will become second nature. Working with type will get easier, and your designs will improve.

right

This poster for a French photography exhibition combines type and image. The visual forms in the type reference the physical forms of the Eiffel Tower and create a tie-in with the image. To connect imagery and concept, try integrating type and image like these designers have done here.

Design: Marko Rašić & Vedrana Vrabec, Zagreb, Croatia

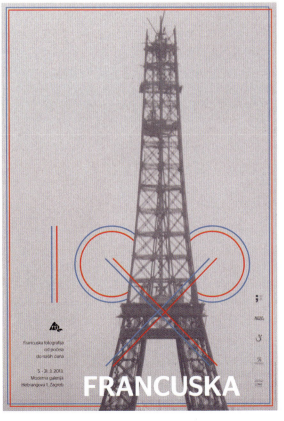

CHARACTERISTICS OF TYPE

Typefaces are classified based on their visual appearance and are divided into major groups according to whether or not they have serifs, and if they refer to calligraphy or another decorative style. This system of arrangement and ordering is called type classification. The most recognized classifications include humanist and old style letterforms that directly relate to calligraphy and were developed in the fifteenth and sixteenth century. Next came transitional typefaces, which have sharper serifs and a more vertical axis than old-style faces. These typefaces formed a bridge between older humanist typefaces and modern serif designs. In the eighteenth and nineteenth century, type design underwent a shift. Serif typefaces were designed on a vertical axis with straight serifs and high contrast of strokes. In the early twentieth century, principles of modernism started to affect type design, and sans serif typefaces were born. Today serif and sans serif faces are both widely used, and there are numerous subcategories of each style described. While there this isn't universal agreement on a single classification system, in upper-level classes you will learn more about the specifics of type and the affect different styles and proportions have on readability. For now it is important to learn to recognize the most common characteristics of different typefaces so you will be able to make better choices when pairing a typeface with text-based information.

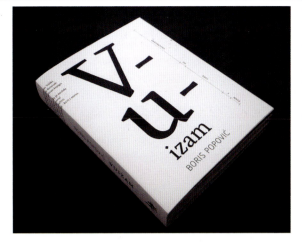

ANATOMY OF LETTERFORMS

x-height—most often the height of lowercase letters, most easily measured with a lowercase x

baseline—line on which the base of each capital letter rests

cap height—the height from the baseline to the top of capital letters

stress—the axis on which a letter is drawn. The axis of on which a lowercase o is drawn is usually used as a way to measure the stress.

terminal—the end of a stroke that lacks a serif

meanline—line that establishes the height of the body of lowercase letters

ascenders—a stroke on a lowercase letter that raises above the meanline

descenders—a stroke on a lowercase letterform that falls below the baseline

serif—small elements added to the ends of the main strokes of a letterform in serifed type styles

sans serif—typefaces without serifs

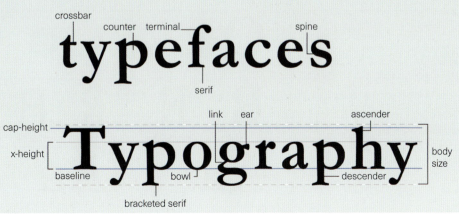

SHAPE AND FORM

The shape of letters can tell you a lot about the typeface they belong to. Individual letterforms are created using a combination of curved and straight lines that form the basis for the more complex shapes. Some letters are more distinct than others. Lowercase o's and e's and uppercase R's provide information about an entire typeface. To practice seeing the unique features of a typeface, ask the following questions.

- Are letters straight or rounded?

- Do letters sit upright or are they slightly skewed?

- Do letters seem to be based on geometric shapes or handwriting?

- Look at the o. Is it round or oval? Is it the same thickness the entire way around or does it get thicker at the sides and thinner at the top? Does the counter (or the space inside the o) mimic the proportions on the outside or does it have its own shape?

- Now look at an uppercase R. Is it wide or narrow? Does the bowl stick way out? Are there serifs on the ends of the stems?

- If the font has serifs what do they look like? Are they tapered or flat or do they end in a decorative shape?

above

Letters have individual shapes, and they can also be customized. Here color and texture are added, and each letter becomes its own composition.

Design: &Larry, Singapore

Is the shape of the letter straight or rounded?	Ee Baskerville	Ee Gill Sans
Do letters sit upright or are they slightly skewed?	Aa Helvetica Oblique	Aa Helvetica
Are the letter forms geometric or do they look like they have been handwritten?	Aa Bodoni Book	Aa Futura
Is the O round or oval? Is it the same thickness the entire way around? Does the counter mimic the proportions on the outside or not?	O o ⎯counter Garamond	O O ⎯counter Gotham
Is the uppercase R wide or narrow? Does the bowl stick out? Are there serifs?	R R⎯bowl Garamond　Rockwell	R R⎯bowl Futura　Univers
If the font has serifs what do they look like? Are they tapered, flat or do they have a decorative shape?	Aa Garamond	Aa Rockwell

WEIGHT

Weight refers to the lightness or heaviness of a typeface and is determined by the ratio of the stroke thickness to the character height. Comparing the weight of individual letters is one of the easiest ways of differentiating one typeface from another or two versions of a font in the same family. Lighter weights are primarily used for text type, whereas heavier weights like bold or black are well suited to headings and display text. Sometimes a very lightweight typeface can be used as display text, but there needs to be enough contrast between the text and the background. The letterforms should be clearly visible when printed or seen on a digital display.

Univers
Bold

Univers
Black

Univers
Light

Univers
Extended

Univers
Roman

Univers
Condensed

Univers
Bold

Univers
Black

left

The Univers family has almost two dozen type styles, so it is easy to use with both light and heavy versions of the same typeface together. Here you can see the difference between bold and black versions of a font.

above

This poster for the Material Art Fair in Mexico City uses a spare, lightweight typeface. Negative space and the spiral shape made by the text draw the viewer into the composition. If you use a lightweight version of a typeface, make sure the text is large enough that viewers are able to read it.

Design: Anagrama, Nuevo Leon, Mexico

MEASURING TYPE

For most of history there was no universal measure for type, but as standardization became more important, a mechanism for measurement developed. Today letterforms are measured by their width using the point system (abbreviated as pt.) and in layouts the measurement pica is commonly used. A pica is 12 points. One of the benefits of using picas is that there are no fractions, which makes measurement easier, particularly when dealing with layout for books, newspapers, and other multipage documents.

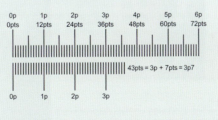

above

Pica is designated with the letter "p," as in 14p or 14 picas. When dealing with parts of a pica, the term is used together with points. 16p4 refers to 16 picas and 4 points.

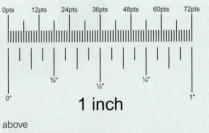

above

Selecting 8 or 10 from a tool palette in the software refers to 8 point type or 10 point type.

TYPOGRAPHIC HIERARCHY

As we already learned, visual hierarchy is the arrangement of elements in a graduated series, from most prominent to least prominent. The primary purpose of text is to communicate information to the viewer. For the viewer to receive the message, you will need to establish a clear visual hierarchy by carefully considering the relative importance of each element in the message and the specifics of the environment where the communication will be seen.

Typographic hierarchy is one of the most important skills students learn because it is the foundation for so many other design decisions. The best way to practice working with hierarchy is to focus on making clear visual distinctions and using the fewest variables to reveal the most information. The fewer variables you use, the more power they have. As you become more comfortable working with text, you can add more visual information while still maintaining the

correct hierarchical arrangement. If too much visual styling is applied to individual elements or an overall composition, hierarchy can be obscured and emphasis will be lost.

One way to determine the correct hierarchy of text is to read the information included in a layout aloud several times. This may feel odd and only works on projects with small amounts of text, but it is helpful nonetheless. Use inflection and volume to emphasize the most important lines or words and a softer voice for less important text. Think about speech patterns. Does the way you are reciting the text mimic the way you would normally show emphasis in speech? If it doesn't, try going back and reciting the text again. This time, stress different parts of the text. Take notes and try a layout based on how you read the text aloud. The result should show clear visual distinctions between text with different communicative content.

below

Scale, color, and placement are used to reveal hierarchy in these promotional pieces for the Swiss-Mexican financial banking firm *Helvetia Trust*. If you used the exercise described in the text to identify the hierarchy, you would read the words *Helvetia Trust* the loudest and *grand opening* and *Zurich Switzerland* second loudest, followed by the supporting text in a quieter voice.

Design: Anagrama, Nuevo Leon, Mexico

REVEALING HIERARCHY

The following variables can be used to order type and reveal hierarchy. By experimenting with each you will begin to understand how to convey emphasis in a two-dimensional space.

Ordering

As we discussed above, the first thing you need to do when working with text is to decide what is most and least important. Make notes or use a colored highlighter to show which lines or words in the text should be seen first, second, and third. This diagram can be used as a map for when and where to apply visual styling to the text.

HER
BIE
HAN
CO&
CKBAND

VINNIE COLAIUTA / JAMES GENUS / LIONEL LOUEKE

26 / 11 / 2014

ZAGREB / KD VATROSLAVA LISINSKOG / 20.30h

Academy Award® winner
14 Grammy Award® winner

above

Hierarchy can be indicated by using different weights of a typeface within the same piece. Notice the difference between the type in the heavier weight and the text in the lighter weight. The size is the same, but weight sets the different pieces of text apart.

Design: Parabureau, Zagreb, Croatia

left

Highlighting text helps identify hierarchy and allows you to group content of similar importance. You can then refer back to the highlighted text when developing a layout.

COFFEE WORKSHOP

The Coffee Shop is hosting our seasonal workshop called Learn to Brew. The classes are held Saturdays & Sundays from October 3rd to November 15th. Sessions are either from 9am-11am or 12pm-2pm. The workshop is located at 64 Driggs Ave, NY, and other details and registration is online at www. Thecoffeeshop.com/workshop.

Perfect for a dates, groups, and for the holiday entertainers. It's a great time to learn a new skill and to bring that perfectly brewed coffee technique to your home. No experience necessary.

COFFEE WORKSHOP

The Coffee Shop is hosting our seasonal workshop called Learn to Brew. The classes are held Saturdays & Sundays from October 3rd to November 15th. Sessions are either from 9am-11am or 12pm-2pm. The workshop is located at 64 Driggs Ave, NY, and other details and registration is online at www. Thecoffeeshop.com/workshop.

Perfect for a dates, groups, and for the holiday entertainers. It's a great time to learn a new skill and to bring that perfectly brewed coffee technique to your home. No experience necessary.

MOST IMPORTANT
SECOND
THIRD

LEARN TO BREW ✓

Oct 3 - Nov 15
Sat & Sun: 9-11 & 12-2

64 Driggs Ave, NY
at The Coffee Shop

Perfect for dates & groups
No experience necessary

Register online:
www.thecoffeeshop.com/
workshop

LEARN TO BREW ✗
Oct 3 - Nov 15
Sat & Sun: 9-11 & 12-2

64 Driggs Ave, NY
at The Coffee Shop

Perfect for dates & groups
No experience necessary
Register online:
www.thecoffeeshop.com/
workshop

LEARN TO BREW ✓

Oct 3 - Nov 15
Sat & Sun: 9-11 & 12-2

64 Driggs Ave, NY
at The Coffee Shop

Perfect for dates & groups
No experience necessary

Register online:
www.thecoffeeshop.com/
workshop

LEARN TO BREW ✗

Oct 3 - Nov 15
Sat & Sun: 9-11 & 12-2

64 Driggs Ave, NY
at The Coffee Shop

Perfect for dates & groups
No experience necessary

Register online:
www.thecoffeeshop.com/
workshop

Space

Space is one of the fastest and easiest ways to separate text and indicate hierarchy. Start by adding a line of space between two lines of text in a block. Having space above and below the first line in the series will make it seem more important.

Weight

Weight is a strong indicator of hierarchy. When working with type, changing one or more lines of type or individual words to a bold or black weight will give them greater prominence.

LEARN TO BREW ✗

Oct 3 - Nov 15
Sat & Sun: 9-11 & 12-2

64 Driggs Ave, NY
at The Coffee Shop

Perfect for dates & groups
No experience necessary

Register online:
www.thecoffeeshop.com/
workshop

LEARN TO BREW ✓

Oct 3 - Nov 15
Sat & Sun: 9-11 & 12-2

64 Driggs Ave, NY
at The Coffee Shop

Perfect for dates & groups
No experience necessary

Register online:
www.thecoffeeshop.com/
workshop

Placement/thresholds

Indenting or moving the threshold of text to one side or the other can provide emphasis and opportunities for grouping information.

left

Terry Tempest Williams

THE WAKE OF BEAUTY

This piece uses multiple thresholds with flush left (see p. 128) orientation and justified body text (see p. 129). The simple system of indents or thresholds accommodates different types of text and produces a clean ordered appearance.

Design: Aufuldish & Warinner, San Anselmo, California

ADDING MORE VARIABLES

Once you have tried using the most basic variables for revealing hierarchy, you can move on to more complex systems of visual signaling. Try using scale and color to further emphasize certain parts of the content. Start by enlarging a single word or a line of text. Then add color to the same word or line. Assess how color and scale alter the appearance of the text. Go back to your original notes on ordering and make sure you have emphasized the correct text. Now combine the principles discussed previously with color and scale and create a new composition. Check your notes on ordering frequently and alter your design to match the hierarchical structure you identified when you first examined the text.

IDENTIFYING OPTIMAL SCALE

Correct scaling of type allows a reader to more easily understand information. Size will also give the reader visual cues about hierarchy. The optimal size for type depends on the distance between the reader and the design and the function of text within an overall composition. Different projects require individual approaches to scale. To see this principle in action, compare a variety of design deliverables. When you hold a book or magazine you are typically no more than 12 to18 inches from the content, and the text can be relatively small. The viewing distance for a street poster or a billboard is greater, and type needs to be larger. Make sure size relationships are noticeable. If you are going to make text bigger, make it visibly bigger. The eye generally has trouble noticing difference of less than two points in size, and minimal shifts in scale may appear to be a mistake or a trick of the eye. Size relationships should be even more pronounced when you are working with display text, pull quotes, or titles. In each case, the display text or heading should be much larger than the body copy.

You have probably been asked to use 12-point text for term papers and other school projects. This size works well for grading papers, but it shouldn't be used as a basis for scaling text on design projects. Twelve-point type is almost always too big for body text in print pieces. Instead, body text is usually set between 9 and 11 points, depending on the characteristics of the typeface. A few points makes a big difference. When body text is too big it will look chunky and out of place. If it is too small it will be hard to read. Look at a few books and magazines. Compare the size of text used

in these objects to one of your old term papers. You might be surprised at how small the text is in the books and magazines. Smaller body text gives the designer more room to accommodate other elements on the page while maintaining visual balance. You can use the same approach on your design projects. Keep body text relatively small and make headings, display text, and other non-standard text bigger. When you are working on a design project, print several versions of text using different typefaces. Then step back and assess how each typeface behaves. This exercise will allow you to see how the shape and proportion of letters affects the overall appearance of a typeface.

above

The front of this kit uses simple visual signaling. Placing the most important text in the center of the composition and making it large helps to reveal hierarchy.

Design: Kuhlmann Leavitt, St. Louis, Missouri

THINGS TO KEEP IN MIND WHEN STYLING BODY TEXT:

1. Sans serif faces tend to appear larger than serif typefaces, but the size variation between two serif typefaces can also be significant.

2. For optimal readability of body text use a font size below 12 text type for body type and above 12 display type.

3. The most readable body text is 9 to 11 point; the exact size depends on the typeface.

4. Sans serif fonts appear larger than serif fonts.

5. Visual weight makes a design more interesting and clearly defines visual hierarchy.

6. Avoid squishing or elongating type. Instead, maintain relative proportions.

This example shows how different point sizes of type can be incorporated into the same piece. As one opens the annual report, the content changes, and so does the size of the body text.

Design: Bruketa&Zinic, Zagreb, Croatia

DIGITAL TYPE

Unlike in print design, the correct scale for body text is more variable when viewing type digitally. Optimal text size is dependent on the size of the user's screen and his/her distance from it. Websites generally use larger size body text than print pieces, but apps use much smaller text because viewers are closer to the screen when they use these devices. On many screens users also have the ability to enlarge and reduce text size. An interactive designer may choose the size of type only to have the user change it later. This lack of control means that establishing initial visual hierarchy is at least as important on the web or on screen-based devices as it is in print.

Clear navigation is essential when working on screen, but it is also helpful to create small chunks of information with accompanying headings. This allows the reader to scan and pick out which pieces of text include relevant information. Use color, lines/rules, and other visual symbols (like arrows or the plus sign) to aid in navigation, and avoid using excessively small body text. When working on screen-based designs, testing is key. Try several iterations of a layout and ask classmates or friends whether they have difficulty reading any screen-based text. Then, if needed, revise the scale and styling of text.

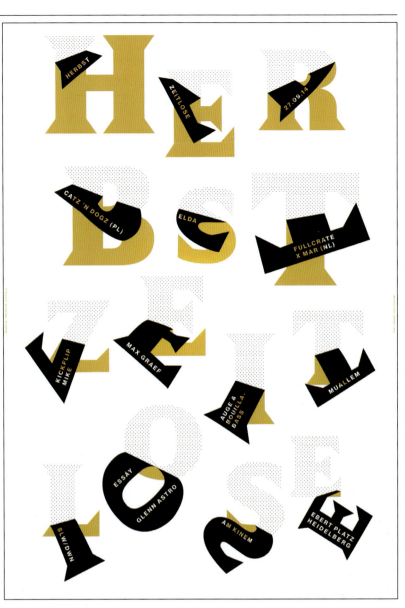

left

Red rules help break up sections of content on this website, and the headings are a larger point size than the other text on the page. The design of this website accommodates the distance the viewer is likely to sit from the screen.

Design: Parabureau, Zagreb, Croatia

above

Type design doesn't have to be static, especially in screen-based designs. Letters bend and fall forward and over themselves in this animated poster.

Design: Goetz Gramlich, Heidelberg, Germany

SPACING AND ALIGNMENT

Letters are almost always seen in groups. The way written language expresses ideas varies depending on what kind of information is being conveyed and who is doing the writing. This fluctuation makes the visual ordering of text unpredictable. Designers use systems for spacing and alignment to ensure text remains consistently readable despite changes in the arrangement of letters, the number of words in lines, and the number of lines in a paragraph. The following arrangement systems will help you style text and can be used to mitigate unusual or problematic characteristics of a particular typeface.

ALIGNMENT SYSTEMS

There are four basic types of alignment. These are flush left, flush right, centered, and justified alignment. Which system of alignment you choose to work with will depend on the type of content being communicated and the format of the design.

The Coffee Shop is hosting our seasonal workshop called Learn to Brew.

The classes are held Saturdays & Sundays from October 3rd to November 15th. Sessions are either from 9am-11am or 12pm-2pm. The workshop is located at 64 Driggs Ave, NY. Other details and registration is online at www. Thecoffeeshop. com/workshop. In this hands-on class, learn all the basics of being a barista: espresso technique, milk steaming, and pouring latte art.

Flush left

Flush left text has been vertically aligned to the left edge of a text block. Flush left alignment is considered the most readable text because viewers read from left to right in most languages. The smooth left margin gives the eye a predictable place to return to after getting to the end of a line. You will need to pay special attention to the right edge of the text block (also called the rag) when working with flush left text. A feathered rag is more desirable than a tight, even rag. Using this system, some lines will be shorter and others will be longer. Flush left text tends to be the easiest alignment system to work with, and it is a good choice if you haven't had practice correctly justifying longer blocks of type.

right

In this design, both the headings and the columns of text use a flush left orientation.

Design: Kuhlmann Leavitt, St. Louis, Missouri

far right

Packaging often uses centered text, but the type on this container of vanilla is flush left, whereas the image is centered in the viewing area.

Design: Rebecca Foster Design, Birmingham, United Kingdom

The Coffee Shop is hosting
our seasonal workshop
called Learn to Brew.

The classes are held Saturdays & Sundays
from October 3rd to November 15th.
Sessions are either from 9am-11am or
12pm-2pm. The workshop is located at 64
Driggs Ave, NY. Other details and registration is online at www. Thecoffeeshop.
com/workshop. In this hands-on class,
learn all the basics of being a barista:
espresso technique, milk steaming, and
pouring latte art.

The Coffee Shop is hosting
our seasonal workshop
called Learn to Brew.

The classes are held Saturdays & Sundays
from October 3rd to November 15th.
Sessions are either from 9am-11am or
12pm-2pm. The workshop is located at 64
Driggs Ave, NY. Other details and registration is online at www. Thecoffeeshop.
com/workshop. In this hands-on class,
learn all the basics of being a barista:
espresso technique, milk steaming, and
pouring latte art.

The Coffee Shop is host-
ing our seasonal work-
shop called Learn to Brew.

The classes are held Saturdays & Sundays
from October 3rd to November 15th. Sessions are either from 9am-11am or 12pm-
2pm. The workshop is located at 64 Driggs
Ave, NY. Other details and registration is
online at www. Thecoffeeshop.com/work-
shop. In this hands-on class, learn all the
basics of being a barista: espresso technique, milk steaming, and pouring latte art.

Centered text

Centered text has a ragged edge on both sides of the text block. Text is aligned at the center of the text block and is symmetrical. Centered text works well for invitations, title or masthead pages, packaging, pull quotes, signage, and some captions and other marginalia. When applied to paragraphs or other longer blocks of type, centered text is difficult to read because there is no consistent threshold. The reader is always searching for the starting point of a line when reading centered text.

Flush right text

Flush right text is vertically aligned on the right edge of a text block. It is the visual opposite of flush left text. Since the left edge of the text is ragged, a viewer has to return to a different place for each line. This makes reading more difficult, and flush right text is not ideal for large blocks of text. Instead this alignment system can be used for small chunks of information such as captions, sidebars, and margin notes, and in situations where numbers and letters need to be accommodated by an ordered system.

Justified text

Justified text is aligned so that both the left and right side of a text block have a smooth straight edge. Justification is the standard for books, magazines, and newspapers because it gives a finished look and uses space efficiently. Since the text is force aligned, justification presents specific styling problems. The most common occurs when white space or "rivers" appear within a block of text. Rivers are formed when there are too few words on a line or when there are several very long words on the same line. Issues with spacing and justification can be overcome by manually tracking words and paragraphs and by force-hyphenating longer words. Learning to justify text well is a skill and needs to be practiced. Avoid including badly justified text in your layouts. It is the mark of an inexperienced designer.

left

Small amounts of text can successfully be set on a flush right threshold, but larger amounts of text tend to be difficult to read when styled this way. Notice how this poster combines centered, flush left, and flush right text orientations.

Design: Studio Beuro, East Sussex, United Kingdom

far left

Large amounts of centered text can be difficult to read, but centered text can be successfully incorporated into layouts when there are only a few lines of type.

Design: Gerwin Schmidt, Munich, Germany

KERNING

Kerning is the space between two or more letters. The shape of each letter in the alphabet is unique, and the amount of space needed to make letters appear to be evenly distributed varies depending on how letters are ordered. Some letter combinations are more problematic than others. Type designers set the kerning for the entire typeface, but the default spacing doesn't work in every situation. Fortunately, users can manually change kerning in design software programs.

Optical correctness trumps numerical correctness. Some letters will need to be closer to each other and others to be farther apart depending on the size of the type and individual attributes of the typeface. Letter combinations including y, o, e, a, and w are particularly problematic, and small caps and capital/lowercase combinations often need special attention. A well designed typeface needs very little kerning when it is scaled for body text, but if the same typeface is used as display text, it is likely to require additional hand kerning.

above

Hand kerning or individually kerning letters is often needed when you use large letters like in this poster. Squint or try turning the design upside down to see if the large letterforms appear to be evenly spaced. If they don't, then you should hand kern them.

Design: Goetz Gramlich, Heidelberg, Germany

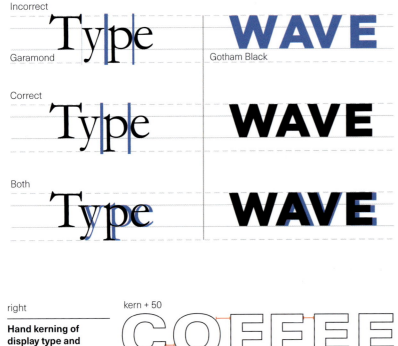

Incorrect

Garamond

Correct

Both

Gotham Black

right

Hand kerning of display type and headings should rely on visual rather than a numerical correctness.

kern + 50

hand kerning

LEARNING TO KERN

A good way to practice kerning is by rotating the text 180 degrees. When the type is upside down and the letters appear primarily as shapes, it will be easier to see problems with letter spacing. The online game KernType can be used on desktops and touchscreen tablets. Users work on kerning progressively more difficult combinations of letters and are scored on their ability to successfully complete each exercise. http://type.method.ac/#

TRACKING

Tracking is the space between groups of letters and should not be confused with kerning, which is the space between pairs of two characters. Tracking is used to space a group of words, lines of type, and even whole paragraphs. There are a number of reasons you may need to increase or decrease the amount of tracking used in a paragraph. If text is has trouble fitting onto a page or in a text box, tracking the text will reduce or increase the amount of space used. Tracking can also reduce the need for excessive hyphenation and eliminate widows and orphans. Lastly, some versions of typefaces may seem too crowded or too open at a particular size, and the text will benefit from being tracked in or out to make the spacing appear to be consistent.

As with kerning, you will have to trust your eyes rather than a particular measurement to achieve well-tracked blocks of text. Generally, kerning and tracking are considered correct if they are imperceptible. For example, if the tracking on a particular paragraph results in crowding of words, too much tracking was probably used. The same is true if there is so much space between letters or words that they seem disconnected. Try to maintain attractive, even spacing by manually adjusting the space between words and letters.

+100 tracking

The Coffee Shop is host-ing our seasonal workshop called Learn to Brew.

The classes are held Saturdays & Sundays from October 3rd to November 15th. Sessions are either from 9am-11am or 12pm-2pm. The workshop is located at 64 Driggs Ave, NY. Other details and regis-tration is online at www. Thecof-feeshop.com/workshop. In this hands-on class, learn all the basics of being a barista: espresso tech-nique, milk steaming, and pouring latte art.

-50 tracking

The Coffee Shop is hosting our sea-sonal workshop called Learn to Brew.

The classes are held Saturdays & Sundays from October 3rd to November 15th. Sessions are either from 9am-11am or 12pm-2pm. The workshop is located at 64 Driggs Ave, NY. Other details and registration is online at www. Thecof-feeshop.com/workshop. In this hands-on class, learn all the basics of being a barista: espresso technique, milk steaming, and pouring latte art.

+ 100 tracking
+ fifty tracking
+ thirty tracking
+ ten tracking
zero tracking
- ten tracking
- thirty tracking
- thirty tracking
- 100 tracking

above

This example shows how too much and too little tracking affect lines of text.

left

For body text or running text, +2 or −2 in tracking is considered undetectable by a viewer and can be used to give a designer more leeway to fit a system. Notice how some of the letters touch or almost touch each other when too little tracking is used.

SPACING IN DESIGN SOFTWARE

Adobe's helpx (http://helpx.adobe.com) includes detailed information and visual examples for different methods for kerning, tracking, and leading in each of the company's software platforms.

LEADING

Leading refers to the space between lines of type. The term dates back to a time when pieces of metal were used as spacers between lines of metal type. Today, leading is set digitally and measured in points. It refers to the space between baselines and can be adjusted in software programs. Some fonts need more leading than others. A font with high ascenders and low descenders will need more space between the lines than an evenly proportioned typeface. Leading is also used to save space on a page and/or make delicate or small type more readable.

The default setting for leading in most software programs is two point sizes larger than body text. Design software allows you to manually set the amount of leading used on a block of text. Test how different iterations of the text work using more and less space and evaluate which is most readable. When you work with small body text (8 or 8.5), try adding one or two extra points of leading to increase readability.

A MISURA DI BAMBINO

allergie e intolleranze alimentari

di Sergio Maria Francardo

Riprendiamo un argomento molto affrontato in questa rivista, ma purtroppo sempre attuale.

Negli ultimi decenni, le malattie allergiche, sia agli inalanti che agli alimenti, sono aumentate in modo formidabile, fino al punto che un cittadino su cinque ne è affetto. Nell'infanzia i dati sono ancora più allarmanti e questo significa che la tendenza è in peggioramento.

Possiamo dire che il benessere economico ha un prezzo che paghiamo fisicamente (si pensi all'evidente parallelismo che esiste tra l'aumento generale dei consumi e quello della carie dentaria).

L'uomo odierno reagisce sempre più spesso con manifestazioni allergiche alla difficoltà di confrontarsi con le sempre più numerose sostanze di sintesi presenti nell'ambiente e introdotte con i cibi. Il proliferare degli stimoli alimentari e la necessità continua di doversi difendere possono condurre a un'eccessiva sensibilità, a modalità reattive di tipo allergen. Va compreso quindi che nell'allergia abbiamo una reazione eccessiva, esagerata

66

Possiamo dire che il benessere economico ha un prezzo che paghiamo fisicamente (si pensi all'evidente parallelismo che esiste tra l'aumento generale dei consumi e quello della carie dentaria).

99

e controproducente ma comunque legata alla necessità dell'organismo di difendersi da sostanze estranee.

Dato per scontato che nell'allergia si manifesta una tendenza costituzionale (la corporeità specifica di quel bambino) e una familiarità (gli allergici nascono facilmente in famiglie di allergici) vorrei proporre alcune riflessioni e indicazioni per ridurre il drammatico emergere dei sintomi latenti della patologia.

Un famoso studio scientifico che riguarda il mondo antroposofico ci mostra delle esperienze positive, come verifico nella pratica clinica.

TRA VITA RURALE E SCUOLA STEINERIANA

Il progetto PARSIFAL (Prevention of Allergy Risk factors for Sensitization in children related to Farming and Anthroposophic Lifestyle) si è occupato di individuare i fattori che potrebbero proteggere da patologie allergiche, analizzando due gruppi di bambini che avevano mostrato una bassa prevalenza di malattie atopiche e sensibilizzazione.

Sono stati coinvolti 14.893 bambini di età compresa fra i 5 e i 13 anni, provenienti da famiglie contadine o frequentanti scuole steineriane, con i rispettivi gruppi di controllo. L'analisi, condotta in 5 nazioni europee (Austria, Germania, Olanda, Svezia e Svizzera) ha previsto la raccolta d'informazioni mediante un dettagliato questionario, oltre alla valutazione degli anticorpi coinvolti nelle allergie (IgE) presenti nel sangue. Malgrado vi siano alcune differenze legate alla specifica nazione, in tutti i paesi esaminati i risultati dimostrano che crescere in un'azienda agricola ha un effetto protettivo nei confronti di rinocongiuntiviti, eczema atopico, asma, sibilo e sensibilizzazione. Anche i bambini che frequentano una scuola steineriana e che conducono uno stile di vita antroposofico mostrano una minor presenza di sintomi allergici e sensibilizzazione, anche se la differenza è meno marcata rispetto a coloro che sono cresciuti in ambiente rurale. Le differenze fra i 4 gruppi di soggetti esaminati si riscontrano anche per quanto riguarda il fattore ereditario, che incide maggiormente nel gruppo della scuola steineriana e nel rispettivo controllo. Probabilmente l'effetto protettivo esercitato dalla crescita in ambiente rurale è dovuto al fatto che i bambini sono esposti fin da piccoli ai microrganismi tipici degli animali da fattoria che, com'è stato dimostrato, proteggono dallo sviluppo di patologie allergiche; inoltre, anche una precoce

39 VALORE ALIMENTARE magazine

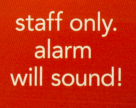

left
_____

Adequate leading ensures that the bottom of ascenders and the top of descenders don't touch in this block of body text.

_____

Design: Bruketa&Zinic, Zagreb, Croatia

above
_____

Even when you only have a few lines of text, it is important to use enough leading so the lines of text appear related to each other but do not seem crowded.

_____

Design: Kuhlmann Leavitt, St. Louis, Missouri

LEADING

The relationship between text size and line spacing or leading is expressed using the word "on." For example, 8 point text with 12 points of leading will be written as 8 on 12.

This page shows examples of tighter and more open leading. Notice how the appearance of the text changes depending on how much space is between the lines of text.

8 on 12

The classes are held Saturdays & Sundays from October 3rd to November 15th. Sessions are either from 9am-11am or 12pm-2pm. The workshop is located at 64 Driggs Ave, NY. Other details and registration is online at www. Thecoffeeshop.com/workshop. In this hands-on class, learn all the basics of being a barista: espresso technique, milk steaming, and pouring latte art.

8 on 15

The classes are held Saturdays & Sundays from October 3rd to November 15th. Sessions are either from 9am-11am or 12pm-2pm. The workshop is located at 64 Driggs Ave, NY. Other details and registration is online at www. Thecoffeeshop.com/workshop. In this hands-on class, learn all the basics of being a barista: espresso technique, milk steaming, and pouring latte art.

8 on 9

The classes are held Saturdays & Sundays from October 3rd to November 15th. Sessions are either from 9am-11am or 12pm-2pm. The workshop is located at 64 Driggs Ave, NY. Other details and registration is online at www. Thecoffeeshop.com/workshop. In this hands-on class, learn all the basics of being a barista: espresso technique, milk steaming, and pouring latte art.

---

7 on 8.5

The classes are held Saturdays & Sundays from October 3rd to November 15th. Sessions are either from 9am-11am or 12pm-2pm. The workshop is located at 64 Driggs Ave, NY. Other details and registration is online at www. Thecoffeeshop.com/work-shop. In this hands-on class, learn all the basics of being a barista: espresso technique, milk steaming, and pouring latte art.

7 on 11

The classes are held Saturdays & Sundays from October 3rd to November 15th. Sessions are either from 9am-11am or 12pm-2pm. The workshop is located at 64 Driggs Ave, NY. Other details and registration is online at www. Thecoffeeshop.com/work-shop. In this hands-on class, learn all the basics of being a barista: espresso technique, milk steaming, and pouring latte art.

7 on 7

The classes are held Saturdays & Sundays from October 3rd to November 15th. Sessions are either from 9am-11am or 12pm-2pm. The workshop is located at 64 Driggs Ave, NY. Other details and registration is online at www.Thecoffeeshop.com/workshop. In this hands-on class, learn all the basics of being a barista: espresso technique, milk steaming, and pouring latte art.

7 on 8.5

Two point sizes larger than the text is considered most common for leading.

7 on 11

With a small type size (8 or 8.5) for body text adding one or two extra points of leading can increase readability.

7 on 7

In extreme cases, the descenders of a typeface will hang down way below the baseline, and the ascenders will extend up from the × height, nearly touching the baseline above. In these instances you will need to add more leading so the ascenders and descenders from above and below don't accidently touch.

LINE LENGTH

The number or words or characters on a line is called line length. Rules dictating line length almost always apply to situations where multiple lines of type appear together. Viewers typically don't read every word on a line. Instead, they scan text and read groups of three or four words. This allows us to assimilate information more quickly. When the line length is too long, readers have difficulty scanning the text. They experience fatigue more quickly and read more slowly. Long line length also affects viewers' ability to read whole paragraphs. They may lose their place or even miss a line as they try to navigate through the text. Long lines of text are awkward, but extremely short line lengths are problematic as well. If text is set in paragraphs and the lines are too short, excessive hyphenation may occur and the rag (or right side) of the text will appear choppy and unresolved.

For optimum readability, nine to twelve words on a line is ideal. If the text size is very small, you may increase the number to twelve or thirteen words; if it is large, nine or ten words works best. A more exact way to measure for line length is to count characters (both letters and spaces). Forty-five to seventy-five characters is considered optimal. Layouts where multiple columns occur on the same page require fewer words or characters per line. In these situations, nine words per line is usually better than twelve. Justified text generally benefits more from longer lines than flush left alignments do. More words help avoid excessive hyphenation and rivers of white space that can occur within paragraphs. For justified text, twelve to fifteen words per line is considered acceptable.

above

This website and application use flush left alignment for the text. Notice how the line length used on the website is slightly longer than what is used for the app. Screen size is an important factor in determining correct line length, especially when you are working on a design for phones and tablets.

Design: B12, Scottsdale, Arizona

right

The relative viewing distance from the design to the audience determines appropriate line length. Optimal line length may vary for different pieces, as we see here with wall displays and freestanding displays. A viewer can read the large type from a distance, but the person is expected to walk up to the displays in order to read the smaller text.

Design: Project Projects, New York

Chapter 5 / Typography

8 pt. The Coffee Shop is hosting our seasonal workshop called
Learn to Brew. The classes are held Saturdays & Sundays
from October 3rd to November 15th. Sessions are either
from 9am-11am or 12pm-2pm. The workshop is located
at 64 Driggs Ave, NY. Other details and registration is
online at www. Thecoffeeshop.com/workshop. In this
hands-on class, learn all the basics of being a barista:
espresso technique, milk steaming, and pouring latte art.

9 pt. The Coffee Shop is hosting our seasonal workshop called Learn
to Brew. The classes are held Saturdays & Sundays from October
3rd to November 15th. Sessions are either from 9am-11am or
12pm-2pm. The workshop is located at 64 Driggs Ave, NY. Other
details and registration is online at www. Thecoffeeshop.com/
workshop. In this hands-on class, learn all the basics of being a
barista: espresso technique, milk steaming, and pouring latte art.

10 pt. The Coffee Shop is hosting our seasonal workshop called Learn to Brew.
The classes are held Saturdays & Sundays from October 3rd to November 15th. Sessions are either from 9am-11am or 12pm-2pm. The workshop is located at 64 Driggs Ave, NY. Other details and registration is
online at www. Thecoffeeshop.com/workshop. In this hands-on class,
learn all the basics of being a barista: espresso technique, milk steaming, and pouring latte art.

14 pt. The Coffee Shop is hosting our seasonal workshop called Learn to Brew.
The classes are held Saturdays & Sundays from October 3rd to November
15th. Sessions are either from 9am-11am or 12pm-2pm. The workshop is
located at 64 Driggs Ave, NY. Other details and registration is online at
www. Thecoffeeshop.com/workshop. In this hands-on class, learn all the
basics of being a barista: espresso technique, milk steaming, and pouring
latte art.

Here the line length is too long.

10 pt. The Coffee Shop is hosting our seasonal workshop called Learn to Brew. The classes are held Saturdays
& Sundays from October 3rd to November 15th. Sessions are either from 9am-11am or 12pm-2pm. The
workshop is located at 64 Driggs Ave, NY. Other details and registration is online at www. Thecoffeeshop.
com/workshop. In this hands-on class, learn all the basics of being a barista: espresso technique, milk
steaming, and pouring latte art.

In this example the columns are too short for the text size. This column width would work well if the type was 4 to 5 points smaller.

14 pt. The Coffee Shop is hosting our   64 Driggs Ave, NY. Other details
seasonal workshop called Learn to   and registration is online at www.
Brew. The classes are held Satur-   Thecoffeeshop.com/workshop. In
days & Sundays from October 3rd   this hands-on class, learn all the
to November 15th. Sessions are   basics of being a barista: espres-
either from 9am-11am or 12pm-   so technique, milk steaming, and
2pm. The workshop is located at   pouring latte art.

NO RULE

The European languages are members of the same family. Their separate existence is a myth. For science, music, sport, etc, Europe uses the same vocabulary. The languages only differ in their grammar, their pronunciation and their most common words. Everyone realizes why a new common language would be desirable: one could refuse to pay expensive translators. To achieve this, it would be necessary to have uniform grammar, pronunciation and more common words.

If several languages coalesce, the grammar of the resulting language is more simple and regular than that of the individual languages. The new common language will be more simple and regular than the existing European languages. It will be as simple as Occidental; in fact, it will be Occidental. To an English person, it will seem like simplified English, as a skeptical Cambridge friend of mine told me what Occidental is.

RULE ABOVE

The European languages are members of the same family. Their separate existence is a myth. For science, music, sport, etc, Europe uses the same vocabulary. The languages only differ in their grammar, their pronunciation and their most common words. Everyone realizes why a new common language would be desirable: one could refuse to pay expensive translators. To achieve this, it would be necessary to have uniform grammar, pronunciation and more common words.

If several languages coalesce, the grammar of the resulting language is more simple and regular than that of the individual languages. The new common language will be more simple and regular than the existing European languages. It will be as simple as Occidental; in fact, it will be Occidental. To an English person, it will seem like simplified English, as a skeptical Cambridge friend of mine told me what Occidental is.

RULE BELOW

The European languages are members of the same family. Their separate existence is a myth. For science, music, sport, etc, Europe uses the same vocabulary. The languages only differ in their grammar, their pronunciation and their most common words. Everyone realizes why a new common language would be desirable: one could refuse to pay expensive translators. To achieve this, it would be necessary to have uniform grammar, pronunciation and more common words.

If several languages coalesce, the grammar of the resulting language is more simple and regular than that of the individual languages. The new common language will be more simple and regular than the existing European languages. It will be as simple as Occidental; in fact, it will be Occidental. To an English person, it will seem like simplified English, as a skeptical Cambridge friend of mine told me what Occidental is.

RULE BETWEEN

The European languages are members of the same family. Their separate existence is a myth. For science, music, sport, etc, Europe uses the same vocabulary. The languages only differ in their grammar, their pronunciation and their most common words. Everyone realizes why a new common language would be desirable: one could refuse to pay expensive translators. To achieve this, it would be necessary to have uniform grammar, pronunciation and more common words.

If several languages coalesce, the grammar of the resulting language is more simple and regular than that of the individual languages. The new common language will be more simple and regular than the existing European languages. It will be as simple as Occidental; in fact, it will be Occidental. To an English person, it will seem like simplified English, as a skeptical Cambridge friend of mine told me what Occidental is.

RULES

Graphic designers use the term "rules" when they are referring to lines. These lines can be thick or thin. They are used in conjunction with type and/or image and are especially helpful when small amounts of text need to be separated from each other or when you need to highlight a single line of text. Rules are placed either below or above a line of type. Adding a rule below a line of text can be problematic if the rule crosses through the descenders of lowercase letters.

above

If used to differentiate or emphasize content, rules should have a clear relationship to the text they apply to. Avoid placing a rule between two lines of type. Instead, the rule should be placed closer to one line than the other.

right

Rules can be thick or thin. Here, heavier, thick rules provide fields for text content and a thinner, lighter rule is used above the navigation on the top to provide emphasis and ground the type on the page.

Design: Project Projects, New York

below

When creating print pieces, the designers used rules to create visual breaks in text content in this book.

Design: Project Projects, New York

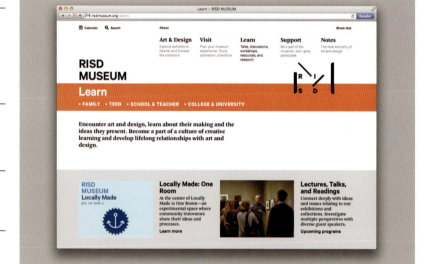

TYPOGRAPHIC NICETIES

Typographic niceties are small styling decisions used make text clearer and easier to read. Talk to practicing designers, and they will have a list of typographic sins that annoy them. Some of the most common are unsightly orphans and widows, unhung quotes (see example at right), rivers in text set using justified alignment, and un-kerned quotations marks at the end of paragraphs. You might think only a designer would notice these details. And you might be right. But every discipline has its own its own set of "insider" rules. People who don't have a background in design might not be able to identify typographic intricacies, but they will appreciate clean, well-designed information. To the art director or senior designer who might one day hire you, typographic niceties are an obsession, so you might as well start focusing on this level of detail while you are in school.

HYPHENATION

Hyphenation is the marked syllabic division of words. It occurs when words are too long to fit on a line and must be broken or separated so that part of the word drops down onto the line below. Hyphens make body text more readable. They allow for a more attractive rag in flush left situations and more successful justification. Hyphenation is considered acceptable when a syllable has three or more letters. Adverbs ending with "ly" and syllables with two or fewer letters should not be hyphenated. Avoid situations where more than two hyphens occur in succession.

PROBLEMS WITH PUNCTUATION

When you style text, punctuation like quotations and bullets should be placed outside rather than within a text block. This system of "hanging" punctuation is considered more elegant than letting the punctuation produce an uncomfortable white space within the text bock. Occasionally production requirements may make it impossible to hang punctuation such as quotation marks or bullets. When this happens, be consistent and adhere to as many typographic niceties as possible.

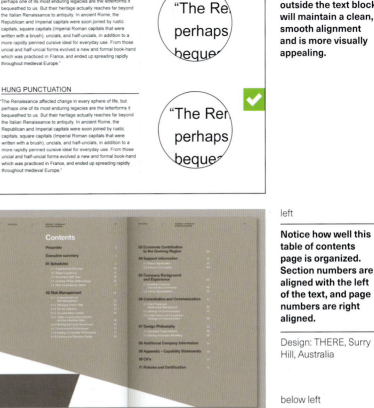

left

Notice how well this table of contents page is organized. Section numbers are aligned with the left of the text, and page numbers are right aligned.

Design: THERE, Surry Hill, Australia

below left

Screen-based design should be just as elegant as print design. Notice how the quotation mark is hung on the outside of the text block.

Design: Aufuldish & Warinner, San Anselmo, California

below

Avoid hyphenating the first two letters in a word as it makes the text difficult to read. Hyphenation of longer words is considered acceptable.

The Coffee Shop is hosting our seasonal workshop called Learn to Brew. The classes are held Saturdays & Sundays from October 3rd to November 15th. Sessions are either from 9am-11am or 12pm-2pm. The workshop is located at 64 Driggs Ave, NY. Other details and registration is online at www. Thecoffeeshop.com/workshop. In this hands-on class, learn all the basics of being a barista: espresso technique, milk steaming, and pouring latte art.

ORPHANS AND WIDOWS

Avoid leaving single words on a line unless they cover at least one-third of the column width. These so-called orphans disrupt the flow of text. Use kerning, tracking, or hyphenation to coax the word up onto the line above or bring a word down to keep the orphan company.

Like orphans, widows occur when a single line of type is by itself at the beginning or end of a column and should be avoided. Break the paragraph so that the widow remains with the previous column or bring two or more lines of type onto the next column or page to accompany the widowed line.

LIGATURES

Ligatures are unique typographic characters produced when two or more letters are joined. Only serif typefaces include ligatures, and they are created exclusively for problematic letter combinations such as double f and the pairing of lower case f and i. Ligatures increase readability and decrease visual tension by avoiding unsightly letter combinations. When a typeface includes with a full set of weights and styles, it will have ligatures as well.

DASHES

Dashes are used to punctuate breaks or pauses and connections between words or parts of sentences. Em dashes indicate a break in a thought and are used instead of colons or semicolons, whereas an en dash is used instead of a hyphen and to indicate a connection between things or names. When working with type you should use the appropriate dash for the grammatical situation rather than hyphens.

Em dashes are as wide as the letter M of the typeface and are created by pressing shift + option + hyphen (—).

En dashes are as wide as a capital N. They are wider than hyphens but not as wide as em dashes and are produced by pressing option and the hyphen key (–).

The Coffee Shop is hosting our seasonal workshop called Learn to Brew. The classes are held Saturdays & Sundays from October 3rd to November 15th. Sessions are either from 9am-11am or 12pm-2pm. The workshop is located at 64 Driggs Ave, NY. Other details and registration is online at www.Thecoffeeshop.com/workshop. In this hands-on class, learn all the basics of being a barista: espresso technique, milk steaming, and pouring latte art.

The Coffee Shop is hosting our seasonal workshop called Learn to Brew. The classes are held Saturdays & Sundays from October 3rd to November 15th. Sessions are either from 9am-11am or 12pm-2pm. The workshop is located at 64 Driggs Ave, NY. Other details and registration is online at www. The coffeeshop.com/workshop. In this hands-on class, learn all the basics of being a barista:

Espresso technique, milk steaming, and pouring latte art.

---

above

Notice the orphans at the end of each paragraph and the widow at the bottom of this example. If you are working with short line lengths, it is acceptable to have a single word on a line if it is at least one-third the length of the line.

right

Ligatures make problematic letter combinations more visually pleasing and less awkward. This example shows two of the most common ligatures, ff and fl.

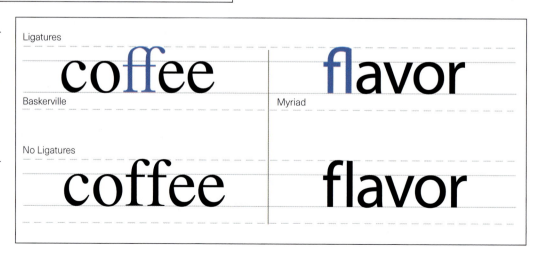

Ligatures

coffee

Baskerville

flavor

Myriad

No Ligatures

coffee

flavor

ORIENTATION AND WORDS

Typically type sits on a horizontal baseline where it can easily be read left to right. But not every typographic expression benefits from horizontal alignment. Signage, book spines, and other design deliverables sometimes use a vertical rather than horizontal alignment, and this can lead to some unfortunate styling decisions. Stacking vertical type seems like a good idea, but it isn't. When letterforms are stacked on top of each other, there will be no consistent alignment point, and the spacing on each side of the letters will be awkward. It is also more difficult to read stacked type. Instead, you should rotate horizontal text ninety degrees clockwise. To see examples of how well this principle works in practice, look at the spines of books on a bookshelf. The text has been rotated rather than stacked, and it is easy to read. Like vertical text, angled text should start on a horizontal baseline and then be rotated to the correct position. When styling lines of type, avoid placing letters one at a time. The result may look more like a ransom note than a piece of graphic design.

TYPOGRAPHIC EXPRESSION

Typographic expression is the styling of text so the visual forms embody or enhance the meaning of the words. Type can be cut, scaled, or distorted. It can also be handwritten or made using unusual objects. You can appreciate the power of typographic expressions by creating your own. In the following exercise you will create visual representations of "active" words.

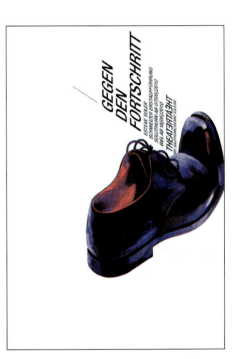

above

The orientation of the type in this poster is considered flush left even though it has been angled.

Design: Stephan Bundi, Boll, Switzerland

left

Sometimes individual lines of type are used to create compositional space. Here are two examples where large letterforms engage with imagery and help break up and delineate space while still forming a readable word.

Design: Bruketa&Zinic, Zagreb, Croatia

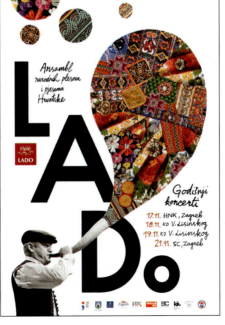

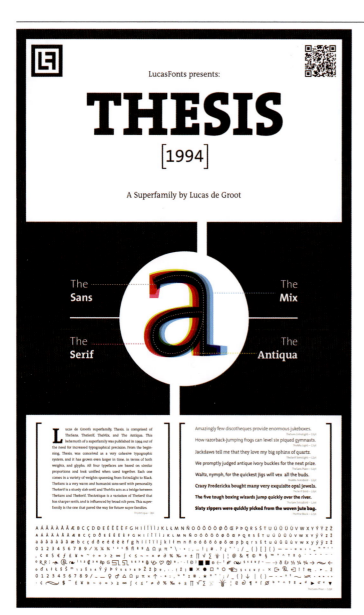

CHOOSING TYPEFACES

Type the words "free fonts" into a search engine and you will find scores of sites advertising hundreds of free typefaces. There are fonts that look like log cabins and cacti. Others have sweeping serifs and dramatic shadows or are characterized by long ascenders and descenders. To further muddy the waters there are hundreds of text faces. Without their serifs and flourishes these typefaces may look remarkably similar to the untrained eye.

While there are certainly some well-designed typefaces on these sites, the adage "you get what you pay for" still has merit. Free fonts aren't always well designed, and they may require more kerning and tracking to appear visually consistent. Free font sites also tend to focus on expressive typefaces, which are better suited to display than body text. Despite all the options, many designers intentionally limit themselves to working with a single font or a few favorites. Others pick typefaces based on the specifics of a job or choose to hand letter or create custom text as needed. When in doubt, work with the tried and true. The typefaces included in this section are popular with professional designers for a reason. Most are available in extended families. Some are more expressive and others are less, but they all have the versatility to work in different situations and with a wide range of content.

above

The typeface Thesis, designed in 1994, has a "super family" and comes with serif and sans serif versions as well as a range of weights. This specimen sheet designed by a student highlights some of the different weights and styles of the typeface.

Design: Michael LaGattuta, New York

right

Zuzana Licko designed Mrs. Eves, the typeface used in this composition, in 1996. It is a revival of Baskerville.

Specimen Sheet Design: Rebecca Brooker, New York

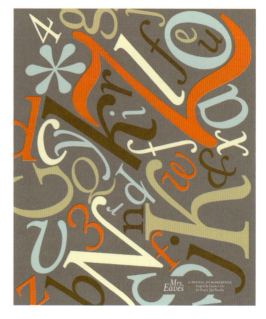

Baskerville

Baskerville is a serif typeface originally designed by John Baskerville in 1724. The typeface is characterized by the contrast between the thick and thin strokes, which gives it an elegant appearance without sacrificing readability.

Bodoni

Originally created by Giambattista Bodoni in 1798, this serif typeface has been reinterpreted many times by different type designers. Bodoni is characterized by un-bracketed serifs and bold strokes, which make it an ideal font for setting blocks of type, and its expressive capitals work well for headings.

Caslon

Adobe's version of Caslon was created by Carol Twombly and is a revival of a typeface originally designed by William Caslon in 1722. Twombly's Caslon is well suited to text type (six to fourteen points) and was designed during her tenure at Adobe Systems.

Frutiger

Designed by Swiss Typographer Adrian Frutiger in 1970, the sans serif typeface bearing his name was originally called Roissy and was designed for signage at Charles de Gaulle Airport. It was later made into a full typeface and given the name Frutiger. It combines the clean sans serif lines associated with Univers (also by Frutiger) with more organic attributes and is well suited for situations where text needs to be seen from a distance.

Futura

Futura is a versatile geometric sans serif typeface designed by Paul Renner in 1927 for the Bauer Type Foundry. Futura's capital letters can be traced to ancient Greek lettering, and Renner's original design underwent significant revision before being released by Bauer.

Garamond

This serif typeface was originally created by Claude Garamond and was used as early as 1530. Since its creation, Garamond has been reinterpreted by numerous foundries and has also been branded with different names including Sabon and Granjon. Garamond is considered one of the most legible typefaces and is particularly easy to work with when setting large amounts of text.

Georgia

Created by Matthew Carter in 1993 for Microsoft Corporation, this serif typeface was designed to be elegant and easy to read even at small sizes and on low-resolution screens. It is still popular for use in screen-based designs.

Gill Sans

Gill Sans is a sans serif typeface designed by Eric Gill for Monotype (type foundry) in 1928. The typeface was designed as a full family and is a good choice when multiple weights are needed. Since it is bundled in both Microsoft Office and the iOS operating system, it is widely available in four most basic styles.

CUSTOM MG FONT

ABCČĆDĐŽĐEFGHIJKLMNOPRSTUVZXYW

above

Working with type: When you want to reference handwriting it is almost always better to write type yourself and digitize it than it is to use a font designed to give the appearance of handwriting. Designers Marko Rašić and Vedrana Vrabec created a custom typeface for this gallery.

right

Creating a typeface by hand: "Moderna sam" means "I am Modern" in Croatian. To develop well-designed handwritten text, you need to practice. It is often helpful to make sketches of the word or phrase first. Then use a tablet to draw a digital version of the text or scan your original drawing and digitize it in a program like Adobe Illustrator. To make a typeface fully functional takes the addition of a more complicated program such as Fontlab (http://fontlab.com).

left

The visual identity for the gallery used elements of the handmade typeface. The letterforms worked well at a variety of sizes and were applied to cups, bags, business cards, and T-shirts.

below

Challenges and solutions: The handmade typeface gave the gallery a distinct visual identity, but it is not readable as body text. When using a decorative typeface, it is often necessary to choose an additional typeface to use when large amounts of text need to be included in design

Biserka Rauter Plančić
ravnateljica / director

Moderna galerija
10000 Zagreb, Hebrangova 1
t:+385 1 60 410 40
f: +385 1 60 410 44
biserka.rauter@modgal.t-com.hr
www.moderna-galerija.hr

TYPE AS FORM

Text can impart information directly, or it can be used to visually represent more abstract ideas. When direct communication is not the primary goal, different expressions of type can provide the basis for layout and can activate and delineate compositional space or provide texture and pattern.

TYPE AS IMAGE

When letters and words are altered so their formal qualities override direct meaning, they can take the place of imagery. This is called using type as image. Individual letters can be enlarged, split apart, cropped, or rotated. Sometimes they become so unrecognizable it is difficult to identify where they originated. These "broken" pieces of text are then added to layouts. The rules for using type as image are similar to working with any other type of text. Avoid skewing, squishing, or otherwise distorting the original shape of the letterforms. It is also usually best to work with cleaner, well-designed typefaces rather than choosing letterforms from already exaggerated or overly decorative fonts.

above

Type is used as the primary visual communicator in this animated GIF. By covering letters with shapes, the message transforms from "we are opening soon" to say "we are open."

Design: &Larry, Singapore

left

The enlarged "b" from the word beautiful helps to create compositional space and is used in place of imagery on the left side of this spread. This is an example of using type as image.

Design: Cheah Wei Chun, CLANHOUSE, Singapore

Chapter 6 / Using and Creating Imagery

CHAPTER 6:
Using and Creating Imagery

KEY TERMS AND CONCEPTS:

Abstraction or abstract images exist with some degree of independence from the natural world and strict representation. (p. 153)

Analog refers to art or design processes that originate with the human hand. Painting on canvas and sculpting clay are analog processes. (p. 164)

Connotation is associated or interpretive meaning. (p. 157)

Copyright is a legal right that gives the originator of an artwork or a design exclusive rights to use or distribute the work within a geographic region and for a given amount of time. Copyright law varies depending on the laws of a particular country. (p. 176)

DPI (dots per inch) is a measurement of the density of pixels or dots in given area and is used in computer-generated graphics. (p. 171)

Denotation refers to direct or literal meaning. (p. 157)

Digital art and design uses technology in its production or distribution. For example, a digital drawing can be created directly with a computer stylus, while a digital print may have originally been created by hand but a computer-based technique is used to reproduce it. (p. 167)

Manipulation in design is the change or alteration of a visual from its original form. Changing color or distorting line quality are both examples of digital manipulation. (p. 172)

Mode is the way an artwork or design was generated. The same subject can be represented using different modes such as photography, drawing, or collage. In graphics software, the "mode" of a file changes what type of color system is used to render it. (p. 158)

Narrative is the story. In design, narrative can be both textual and visual. For example, imagery and other visuals can be used to complement or refer to particular aspects of the text, or simple shapes may be used on their own to create a visual narrative. (p. 152)

Permissions or photo release is a legal release or waiver signed by a model (for photography) or by the originator or owner of an artwork granting another person the permission to publish or reproduce the photograph or artwork. (p. 176)

Pixilation refers to digital or digitized imagery that has been enlarged or distorted so the image breaks up and individual pixels can be seen. Pixilation of imagery should generally be avoided. (see *Image Formats* p. 168)

Representational images are images that are clearly recognizable and refer to life. For example, a representational image of a dog will look similar to how the dog appears in life. (p. 155)

Semiotics is the study of signs and symbols and how meaning is created and communicated. (p. 157)

Stock images are sold by companies (usually online) for use in creative projects. Stock image sites may charge a fee depending on the specifications of the intended use, or one can buy a subscription allowing the use of any images on the site. Stock sites sell photographic imagery, digital imagery, and some video footage. (p. 159)

Style is the appearance or distinctive visual character. An image may be drawn in either an abstract or representational style, for example. (p. 158)

THE IMPORTANCE OF IMAGERY

People "see" and understand visual content more quickly than they do text. This makes imagery a crucial tool for communicating a message. Designers combine imagery and other elements to express concepts, convey emotion, and provide visual interest. How well images work within a project will be determined by the style of the image, how well it complements the text, and whether it correctly targets the intended audience. Like every other visual, imagery exists as form in space. Regardless of how visually powerful an image is on its own, it needs to be incorporated into a composition so that it maintains the appropriate hierarchy with the other elements of the design.

Images are developed using a variety of media and processes, and they function differently depending on the needs of a project. Advertisements often use full-color photographs to quickly get a viewer's attention, whereas identity marks are less complex and are often developed using simplified visuals that have been created in software like Adobe Illustrator. Images differ in appearance depending on how they are generated and the degree to which they reference life. Illustrations are not usually as realistic as photographs, and paintings and collages may further abstract or interpret the subject matter. Images can be made by hand using art-making techniques, produced with a camera, or created directly in computer software using a mouse or stylus. Designers use images as the focal point of a composition, to create a visual narrative, or to complement or clarify text content. Images can also be used as a background or as a decorative element rather than as a way of communicating content. The type of image that is most appropriate will be determined by the context in which it is to appear, the expectations of the target audience, and the stylistic goals of the project.

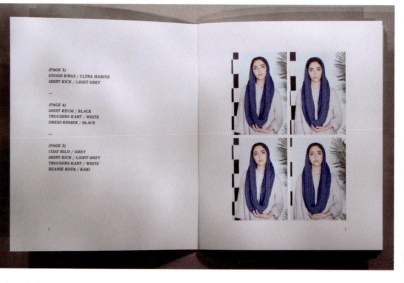

left and above

Designers often choose from a variety of images when developing layouts. This example shows several images from a photo shoot and then the resulting layout with two of the images used in the design.

Design: Acme, Paris, France

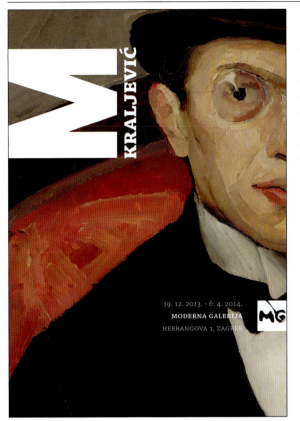

above

Imagery isn't always photographic. Here a painting provides the focus for this book cover for an art exhibition.

Design: Marko Rašić & Vedrana Vrabec, Zagreb, Croatia

REPRESENTATION AND ABSTRACTION

An image is considered representational when it portrays a subject that has a physical reality, regardless of whether the image is produced using photography, illustration or painting. Representational images are a mainstay in design, and they are ubiquitous in advertising where direct visual associations are commonly used as a persuasive tool. When an ad tells the viewer to "use this shampoo for healthier and shinier hair," a high-resolution image of a model with beautiful hair is not only the most obvious pairing, it is also likely to be the most successful. Generally, representational images are used to emphasize a particular idea or to literally symbolize content. However, imagery and meaning exists on a continuum between pictorial representations and associated or abstract depictions. In other words, as a visual becomes less pictorial and more abstract, the meaning associated with that image will become less literal, and different interpretations can be applied.

right

This example shows how the appearance of an image changes as it becomes more abstract.

Photographs with and without people in them are used to advertise this cologne. In the second example, the water provides context and a background for the image of the product. In both instances, the photos are representational.

Design: Seitaro Design Inc., Tokyo, Japan

Just because representation is the most commonly used format doesn't mean it is right for every situation. Some projects will benefit from visual ambiguity. To achieve less direct communication, you should look for abstract visuals or imagery that is textural or made up of a pattern. Distorted or blurry photos and illustrations might seem like an odd choice, but their lack of a direct meaning allows for a wider interpretation. The originator may create his/her own abstract imagery or might use found material such as old magazines or bits of fabric, for example, and alter or repurpose them to fit the design. By distorting a visual beyond recognition, a designer is able to harness the visual impact of an image without having to directly match its original meaning to the text content. When the direct meaning has been obscured or decreased, it is possible for new ideas to be applied or associated with the image.

Deciding when to try abstract imagery in a project can be challenging. You should consider whether the message you want to communicate would benefit from a direct visual reference, for example, as in the shampoo ad we discussed earlier, and if there are images readily available to match or enhance the text content. If there are no obvious visuals to go with the content or if a more subtle visual solution is the goal, then abstract imagery might be a good choice. It is worth trying several iterations of the design with and without representational imagery, keeping in mind that compositions created with simple forms and type may be just as successful as those that use either representational or abstract imagery.

Pictorial or representational images reference the physical world and have literal meaning associated with them. Representational images work best when direct meaning is required.

Abstract images are less direct and do not reference the physical world. Abstract images are useful when type content is dominant, in situations where no obvious subject exists, or when the designer wants to create a non-specific visual texture. For an example of greater and lesser abstraction see page 153.

above left

The images used on this website are representational. They show the texture and color of the cloth. When designing a website without a lot of text content, imagery can be used to visually tell the story of the company.

Design: &Larry, Singapore

left

This brochure for a high-end nail salon includes distorted repeated photographic imagery and gives the layout an edgy appearance.

Design: Lotta Nieminen, New York

above

This painting is an example of a representational image. By rendering the figure realistically, the artist has directly referenced life and his subject.

Artist: Mike LaGattuta, New York

REDUCTIVE IMAGE FORMS

Sometimes simple graphics work better than more complex imagery and are often understood more quickly. Since icons, symbols, and pictograms quickly communicate ideas, these forms of images are used for logos, on road signs, and in airports. Once you learn the system of association, the meaning of symbols can be transferable depending on the context. Symbols and icons are usually made up of simple lines and shapes. Pictograms may be slightly more complex, but they don't include as much visual information as an illustration.

Icons

Icons are visual forms used to represent a person, object, or an idea. They are immediately recognizable and are produced by reducing a visual to its simplest form. The benefit of icons is that they don't include any distracting details. Icons are used for logos and signage and to aid in navigation on websites and smartphone and tablet applications.

Symbols

Symbols are graphic representations of ideas or concepts that exist without pictorially describing what they relate to. Companies use symbols to represent their brands even when the visual doesn't directly relate to the goods or services produced by the company. Nike's swoosh is immediately recognizable even though it doesn't directly represent clothing or shoes. Similarly, Target's bull's-eye, McDonald's arches, and Walmart's smiley face are easily associated with the companies' brands even though the visuals don't describe the goods being sold. Because of their nonspecific form, the same visual symbol can be used to represent more than one object, person, or idea. For example, the Nazis used the swastika as a visual symbol for fascism even though the same form had been used by Hindu and Buddhist cultures where it represented well-being.

below

Visuals become recognizable when they are associated with brands or organizations.

right

This identity for the "groovy goddess" uses shapes that look like the letter "g" and another abstract shape to represent the head. The visual form ends up being evocative without being too specific.

Design: B12, Scottsdale, Arizona

right

Look at the difference between these two sets of icons. Each set uses a consistent visual language, but one set is rendered with clean lines and the other references pixelization.

Design: B12, Scottsdale, Arizona

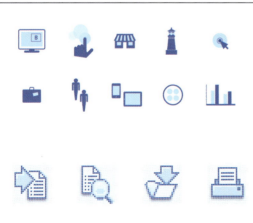

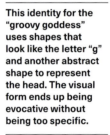

ingressus viridis

above

Simple shapes can be put together so they become symbols that can be associated with an organization or cause. Using abstract shapes is a good choice when you don't want to directly illustrate the function or product produced by a company.

Design: Marko Rašić & Vedrana Vrabec, Zagreb, Croatia

Pictograms

Pictograms (or pictographs) are representations of a letter, word, phrase, or physical concept. They rely on a viewer's ability to make an association between a visual and what it represents. Early writing is thought to have developed out of pictograms, and evidence of the direct visual associations between imagery and ideas is still found in some characters in the Mandarin alphabet. The designs used to indicate men's or women's toilets are pictograms with which most of us are familiar. Pictograms can transcend cultural and language barriers because they are universally recognizable and are often used as a communicative device in places where a large percentage of the population is illiterate.

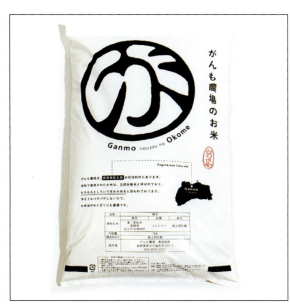

SEMIOTICS

You may hear about semiotics in an art history or design class and wonder what it means. The term sounds more complicated than it is. Semiotics is the study of how meaning is created and is communicated through signs and symbols. In semiotics, understanding and interpretation are broken down into several stages. First, a person sees or becomes aware of a sign, symbol, or visual. This stage is called perception. Then, in the manipulation stage, the viewer interprets the sign and considers how to respond. Finally, in consummation, the viewer responds to the visual.

Semiotics is based on the following assumptions. Every sign or symbol has meaning. More than one meaning can be ascribed to the same visual, and these interpretations are influenced by culture and the subject's or interpreter's previous experience. Two other terms associated with semiotics are connotation and denotation. Connotation is associated or interpretive meaning. Essentially, it is understanding based on experience and ideas the subject already possesses. For example, if you have seen a road sign in the past you will think the next similar road sign you see probably has the same meaning even if you are in a different country. Denotation is more literal; it refers to the direct meaning of a visual without the influence of the interpreter's feelings or personal ideas about what the image suggests.

Semiotics is important to graphic design because designers are always trying to communicate a particular message to an audience. Understanding how the audience or subject is likely to react to an image or sign and acknowledging that the subject may bring his/her own associations to any understanding of your message will help you evaluate visual work and assess the likelihood of inspiring the intended action or understanding in the viewer.

left

The design of a rice bag for Ganmo Farm in Japan uses a visual form that is reminiscent of pictographs.

Design: Seitaro Design, Inc., Tokyo, Japan

below left

Different versions of bathroom icons show how much variation occurs even in simple forms. Because these symbols are so common, a viewer or subject will understand what is being communicated despite the differences in how the figures are rendered.

Design: Kuhlmann Leavitt, St. Louis, Missouri

MODES AND STYLE

The mode of an image refers to the media or technique used to produce it. When combined with style, the mode will affect the literal meaning as well as any interpretations a person has when viewing an image. For example, a photograph will elicit a different reaction from the viewer than a line drawing of the same subject. Similarly, a simple contemporary-looking illustration will engender a different interpretation than an ornate historically based version of the same subject. Before presenting an image, the designer needs to consider what message is being conveyed and whether the visuals should function literally or can evoke associated meaning. If a literal interpretation is needed, then representational or pictorial imagery such as a photograph or realistically rendered illustration will be most suitable. For situations where an interpretive meaning is more appropriate, a visual that has been obscured or abstracted in some way or that contrasts with the text content can be quite effective. Combining more than one style or mode of visual material offers the opportunity to extend or alter meaning and change the visual language of the entire composition. A photograph paired with abstract visuals such as texture or a pattern can work well, but there should be a clear purpose to the grouping.

left

Pen and ink illustrations make individuals in the "about the staff" section of this recruitment brochure seem approachable and unique, whereas a similar photo might have seemed static or too obvious.

Design: Seitaro Design Inc., Tokyo, Japan

above

Photographs and bright colors create a narrative of wealth and luxury for this real estate brochure. By using photography, the designer makes a very direct reference to a physical place and invites the viewer to imagine him/herself there.

Design: THERE, Surry Hill, Australia

- Evaluate what type of visual material will communicate the message best (e.g., photography or illustration) and the style, look, or degree of representation or abstraction most suited for the project. Illustration and line art are sometimes more appropriate than photography because these forms can be rendered so they avoid direct association with a subject. For instance, a photograph of a little girl will obviously portray a specific individual, whereas a line drawing can be rendered more generally so the viewer understands "little girl" rather than "Sally."

- Consider the intended audience and whether one type of image may appeal more or less to the targeted group.

- Evaluate whether there are special production issues that need to be considered (e.g., whether the final output will be seen online or in print). For example, if you are working on a billboard or large outdoor banner, the image resolution must be very high so that it doesn't pixelate.

- Decide whether the composition and content will benefit from a single image or whether it is appropriate to use multiple images in the project.

- Do you have a tight budget? If so, try using low-cost stock images that can be found online or creating them yourself.

- Are there cost or copyright issues to consider (see p. 176)?

- Consider the tone of the message and whether imagery should be dominant or whether it should take a more subordinate role in the composition.

STOCK IMAGES

For decades stock images got a bad rap because they often appeared staged or overly dramatic. Today online providers have a multitude of images available to designers at a range of prices. Some of the images can still be a bit cheesy and overly staged, but many sites also allow amateur and professional photographers and illustrators to upload a wide variety of visual material. Many of these sites also sell illustration, vector art, and even video clips. Stock sites cater to every budget. Media and design companies commonly purchase subscriptions to these services, but there is enough of a range in price so that even students can afford low-cost or free stock imagery. Your instructor may stipulate that you have to generate imagery yourself, so be sure to check if it is okay to purchase images or use someone else's work before using this type of visual material in design projects.

left

These collages use found imagery in unexpected ways. Consider using collage when you want to create your own unique and original visual for a project.

Design: Katie Mias, New York

APPLYING ART-MAKING TECHNIQUES TO DESIGN

Even though the goals of art and design may be quite different, the processes and media normally associated with fine art can provide a rich source of visual material that you can use in graphic design problem-solving. After having taken classes in art-making, you may still be unsure how to incorporate these techniques into your design assignments. By assessing your ability in a given media and evaluating the facilities at hand, you should be able to identify which fine art practices might work for a design project. Begin by noting whether you have the equipment you need to work in a particular area and whether you have expertise in that medium. For example, if printmaking is one of your skills, do you have access to a printing press, or if you take photos in your spare time can you save them for use in school assignments? Some people excel at representational drawing, while others may be more skilled at collage or photography. Each of these methods can be applied to design projects, but it is often easier to begin by using techniques you are already comfortable with. If no art-making facilities are available, consider focusing on digital photography, collage, or another medium that doesn't require specialized equipment.

It is important to honestly evaluate whether handcrafted or self-initiated material is appropriate for your project. Think about who the target audience is and the content being communicated. Ask yourself whether the message will be conveyed more effectively with less traditional forms of imagery. If the answer is no, then look for more conventional sources for obtaining images, such as stock image sites or picture libraries. Just because you haven't seen a particular solution used in similar projects doesn't mean it won't produce a successful result. Experimentation and risk-taking are an important part of the design process, and you should strive to break new ground and create unusual and/or unique work whenever possible.

above

Illustrations don't need to be realistic or highly rendered. Even sketches can help create a visual narrative and make text content more engaging, as was done in this book design.

Design: Bruketa&Zinic, Zagreb, Croatia

HOW TO CHOOSE WHETHER TO USE SELF-GENERATED IMAGERY

- Assess how visual material will be used in the compositional space and whether images need to be customized to work with the other elements.

- Can two or more images or types of media be combined to produce a collage using targeted visuals?

- Can you or a member of the design team produce the imagery needed for the project? If not, try partnering with an illustrator or photographer.

DRAWING AND ILLUSTRATION

Drawing and illustration offer countless possibilities for using custom visual material in design projects. In some cases, realistic renderings may easily complement text and emphasize the message, but abstract expressive drawing can also be effective, as can drawings using a cartoon style. Since a drawing need not be bound by the limitations of reality, you are free to enlarge, reduce, or distort individual details to enhance particular features or qualities of an object. The same subject can be represented using different styles. A technical drawing of a plant will include every detail of the petals and leaves, whereas a looser pen and ink drawing might only use a few strokes to give an outline to the overall form. If eyes, nose, and mouth are drawn onto the plant, then it will become a character.

There are appropriate applications for each style of drawing, but it's important to choose one that will complement the content and be targeted toward a specific audience. For example, the cartoon of the plant described above might not be appropriate for a bank advertisement, but it would be a great visual to

go on a snack pack of veggies aimed at school-age children. A designer should assess how meaning shifts when drawings are produced using different tools. When creating illustrations, it is best if you can develop multiple versions of an illustration and experiment with a variety of media and/or types of line quality. You can then test the various versions in the composition and evaluate how effective each version is in enhancing the communicative content, correctly targeting the intended audience, and working well in the context where the final piece will be seen.

left

Unlike the example of the bakery packaging above, the illustration used for these wine labels is not representational. Instead, the design uses more of a cartoon style and is humorous rather than elegant.

Design Eduardo Bertone, Madrid, Spain

above

Delicate illustrations of flowers provide continuity, color, and a specific visual style when used to create this identity system for a bakery. If you are good at drawing, try adding one or more handmade elements to an identity design to create a custom visual for the client or for a school project.

Design: Anagrama, Nuevo Leon, Mexico

EXERCISE:
Everything is a Remix
Courtesy of Liz DeLuna

Poster design demands immediacy, graphic impact, and clarity. In this project you will explore the relationship between found images and concepts. The assignment is to create a poster for the movie *Everything Is a Remix*. Begin by watching the short segments of the movie and making notes on what the film is about and the content and tone of the film. Then do quick online research. Read several reviews of the movie and find out who made it and why.

Part One: Collage

Create two initial non-digital collages on the theme of REMIX. Your compositions should be a response to the video series: http://everythingisaremix.info/watch-the-series/. These collages will become the foundation for your poster and online advertising designs. This exercise works well as a group project, but you can also do this on your own.

Specifications:
Size: 8 × 12 inches

Required materials: Scissors, X-Acto or matte knife. Cutting mat. Glue stick, rubber cement, bookbinding glue, or another non-water-based glue. Board for the background and materials to create the collage.

Optional materials: Magazines, newspapers, books, photographs, fabric, string, images printed from the internet and/or your own drawings, pens, paints, colored pencils, ink, and brushes.

1. Take a look at the materials you have collected and review your notes on the movie segments. Come up with several concepts for how subtopics or taglines might be expressed visually. Once you have developed a few ideas, begin to cut out images and set aside textures or other materials. Make sure you consider the edges. Images can be cut cleanly or purposely torn.

2. Create one or two test compositions without pasting items on the board. This will allow you to move pieces around. Try altering your compositions so that more negative space is used and some elements extend beyond the edges and or are cropped at the edge of the composition. Once you are satisfied, glue the items to the board.

Part Two: Poster

Using your collage elements, create two posters and/or online advertisements for *Everything Is a Remix*. You can use these elements in any way that you choose to create your designs. You can scan them, photograph them, or cut them up digitally or physically. Supporting text can be set digitally; you can create a collage using found type or you can draw the text by hand.

Specifications:
Print: Posters should be 20 × 30 inches full color. Posters can be created in Adobe Illustrator, Photoshop or InDesign.

Text to include:
Presenting
Everything is a Remix
A Film by Kirby Ferguson
June 5, 2018
IFC Film Center, 323 Sixth Avenue, NYC
www.ifccenter.comhttp://everythingisaremix.info/

Digital: Create at least one leader board and rectangular advertisement. The designs should be complementary so they can be seen together on the same site/page.
Leader board: 728 × 90 pixels
Large rectangle: 336 × 280 pixels
Half page: 300 × 600 pixels

Text to include:
Everything is a Remix
A Series of Short films
by Kirby Ferguson
@remixeverything
http://everythingisaremix.info/

Note: The goal of this exercise is to demonstrate how visual decision-making changes when you work with analog materials and make compositions by hand. This exercise will not produce the same results if you start working directly on the computer.

PRODUCING IMAGES DIGITALLY

One of the most common ways of producing images digitally is to use a mouse or track pad on a laptop or a tablet with a stylus to input lines directly into a program like Photoshop or Illustrator. These tools produce visual material that retain evidence of the originator's hand while still being easy to edit and scale by using computer software. Specialized applications for tablets and smartphones enable artists to draw directly on the screen, and you can use styluses with different tips to achieve varied line quality, but if you take your time you can use a mouse and achieve nearly the same results.

If your rendering skills are not that good, another method for producing digital images is using tracing. The artist or designer begins by making a sketch or line drawing by hand. Then the image is scanned into the computer to produce a digital file and is imported into Adobe Illustrator. Using the mouse or track pad and the pen tool in Adobe Illustrator (or a similar program), it is possible to trace over the scanned image. If you use this technique you may have to practice with the pen tool since the way it renders curves and points is somewhat counterintuitive (see Bezier curves p. 68). It is also possible to trace a scanned image using the paintbrush tool and/or the pencil in Adobe Illustrator or Photoshop. While the paintbrush and pencil tools may seem easier at first, they rarely produce the same line quality as the pen tool, and the imagery may have a very "computer-generated" appearance.

LIVE TRACE

The Live Trace option in Adobe Illustrator allows a user to take a black and white scanned raster image and change it into a vector file.

Users can customize the way information is converted through the Tracing Options dialog box. Unless one uses the tool skillfully, Live Trace creates visually predictable results similar to those produced by Photoshop filters. Many instructors prefer you to input your own lines using the methods described above. Check with your instructor before using Live Trace, and if you do use this technique, make sure you assess whether the lines resulting from a trace look like they could only have been produced in Adobe Illustrator. If this is the case, consider going back and editing the trace settings and/or tracing the image with the pen tool instead.

above

The illustrations of animals, fruit, and the logo for this student project were produced using a stylus and tablet; however, the same results could have been achieved using the pen tool in Adobe Illustrator.

Design: Jessica Monteavaro Garbin, New York

CUSTOM PHOTOGRAPHY

Photographs are almost unrivalled in their ability
to quickly communicate ideas and tone. They are a
mainstay in advertising design, where they are used to
make products more desirable, but they are also used
in almost every other form of design work. Professional
designers hire photographers to ensure that images
correctly convey the desired concept and meet
high-quality technical standards, but you don't need a
photography studio or expensive equipment to produce
images to use in design projects. You can shoot the
images yourself with a digital camera, smartphone,
or disposable camera. Taking an intro class in digital
photography will make the process easier, but is not
required. Remember, even great photographers take
dozens of images before identifying the best photo.
You should do the same. If you are shooting a live
scene or a person, take several photos from a variety of
angles. When setting up staged interior photo shoots,
try altering the light source, working with a backdrop,
or rearranging props and models. Always take high-
resolution photos since you can easily reduce the
resolution but cannot increase it. Once you have a
variety of images to work with, you may want to crop
the images and to adjust the contrast and color balance
before settling on the ones that are most suitable to
include in a design layout.

Not every design project will require custom
photography. Sometimes a more general image will
suffice. In such cases, consider looking online for
visual material and check out stock sites (see p. 159) or
look for free or low-cost visual material in magazines
or newspapers.

above

You might think you
have to choose between
photography and illustration
when working on design
project. In fact, you can use
both together as long as the
elements are balanced and
work well when they are
seen together. The designers
of these cookie packages
used photography of the
cookies and an illustration of
the teacup in a single unified
composition.

Design: Metalli Lindberg,
Treviso, Italy

right

If you work in editorial design
you may have the opportunity
to participate in professional
photo shoots such as those
for Glam magazine. The
benefit of working with
commercial photographers is
their ability to produce many
high-quality visuals.

Design: Cheah Wei Chun,
CLANHOUSE, Singapore

WORKING WITH THREE-DIMENSIONAL OBJECTS

Building or finding three-dimensional props is another easy, low-cost way to develop customized visual content to use in your design projects. There are numerous methods for incorporating three-dimensional items in design layouts. You can set up a scene on a tabletop using three-dimensional objects or cut-outs and then photograph them. Children's toys can be put into unusual scenarios, you can cut out figures and place them in a diorama, or create small sculptures and photograph them in a real-life setting.

Finding props is like going on a treasure hunt. You can look among objects you already own, find items in thrift stores, look for things people have thrown out, or fabricate props using cardboard, clay, or other art-making supplies. Don't feel limited by traditional materials. String, food, masks from a costume store, and even discarded refuse can all be used as raw material for 3-D image-making. In most cases, a prop will have to be photographed either in a given scenario or on a white background, which can easily be "cut out" in a photo-editing program like Adobe Photoshop.

Using found objects and handmade props isn't difficult, but it can be time-consuming, so if you have a short turnaround time or lack the facilities to properly photograph items, you might want to reconsider using them. To use this type of material successfully in your design project, you usually need to have a strong concept or story line before you start.

HOW TO INPUT ARTWORK OR 3-D OBJECTS INTO THE COMPUTER

Two-dimensional artwork or other material

Option 1. Scan two-dimensional artwork at 300 dpi or greater depending on the final size of the layout. For on-screen projects scale down the images to 72 dpi after scanning.

Option 2. For two-dimensional work, take photographs outdoors using natural light or use a copy stand if your school has one. Stand above the work or put the camera in the designated position (on the copy stand) so you can shoot the entire piece without distortion, but make sure you aren't casting a shadow that can be seen in the photo. Take at least three shots to ensure that the focus and the angle are correct.

Three-dimensional objects and props

Use an interior table-top set up. If possible, use a three-point light system: one overhead light, and two spotlights set at forty-five degree angles to the piece. Shoot at the highest resolution allowed by your camera and then edit and size the images in a photo-editing program.

If you are shooting a three-dimensional object or diorama, you may need to experiment with several lighting arrangements before finding the one that accurately represents the scene.

left

This event flyer used a cropping of a photograph of a handmade string composition. The physical piece was photographed at several different angles and with a variety of lighting sources before the designer chose one image to use as the basis for the composition.

Design: Bianca Alcantara, New York

far left

These shears were photographed, cropped, and added into this composition to create the shape for the head of the figure shown in this poster. Try using 3-D objects like these as a way to create custom visuals for your design projects.

Design: Stephan Bundi, Boll, Switzerland

Original

Low Contrast

B & W

Monotone

Color Dodge

Extreme

above

This example shows how an image appears when it has been manipulated with a different Photoshop filters and effects. As you can see, some of the effects like "extreme" exaggerate the color to the point that the image looks over-manipulated.

TIPS FOR MANIPULATING IMAGERY

1. Start with high-resolution, good quality images. (see p. 159 for info about sourcing imagery).

2. Decide how the visual material needs to be altered before you begin.

3. Strive to enhance an existing image rather than apply a "cool looking" effect.

4. Avoid filters that reference art making. If you want an image to look like it was painted or drawn, start with an actual painting or drawing rather than using a built-in effect.

5. Avoid tricks of the eye. Photoshop tutorials often use visual illusions to teach ways of working with the program. Tutorials are an excellent way to learn software, but the techniques being taught are not always appropriate to use in design work.

6. Ask yourself whether it is obvious that an image was manipulated using a computer program. If it is, consider going back to the original and reducing the number of filters or blending modes.

7. Evaluate whether a manipulated image works well with other elements in the composition, is appropriate for the audience, and supports the overall message of the project.

Note: Many illustrators and designers use a combination of drawing and digital manipulation to produce original engaging visuals. There is nothing intrinsically wrong with digital manipulation. The most common filters and blending modes are simply overused.

WORKING WITH IMAGES

Before working on an overall layout composition, the designer needs to evaluate each image for how it will fit and whether the image should exist in its original form or would work better if were cropped, altered, distorted, or manipulated in some way to clarify or obscure meaning. Cutting up, repeating, or modifying an existing image can produce new visual material or enhance what already exists. Design software includes tools for altering imagery, but if you are working with analog or found visuals, some of the editing and alteration of images can be done by hand.

DIGITALLY MANIPULATING AND EDITING IMAGES

Digitally manipulated images can originate as photography, illustration, or scanned textures, and they may start out either in digital or analog form. Software like Adobe Photoshop and Illustrator includes a variety of options for manipulating images. Built-in tools can lighten or darken images, distort or skew images, and produce a range of affects with blending modes, filters, and other options. Image manipulation tools provide numerous choices for designers, but there are inherent dangers when using these techniques. Because the software makes altering images relatively simple, it is easy to overuse the filters and blending modes built into Adobe Photoshop and Illustrator. It is usually best to follow the adage "less is more" and simply enhance what already exists rather than rely on the software to make a poor image better or create an unusual visual effect. Remember, everyone who uses these software packages has access to the same tools. A good rule of thumb is to ask whether it is obvious an image was manipulated. If it is, consider whether it is evident which tools were used to make the alterations. If the answer to either of these questions is yes, consider going back to the original image and reducing the manipulation. In most cases, however, it's better to start with high-quality visuals rather than relying on the software to produce a particular "manipulated" appearance.

The client: West Elm is an upscale retail store that sells contemporary furniture designs, housewares, and other products. To create a collection of fitness products, West Elm partnered with The Fitness Guru, a personal trainer and gym brand dedicated to putting fun back into health and fitness.

The brief: The two companies decided to work together to create a vintage collection of fitness products including dumbbells, jump rope, yoga mat, towels, and a gym bag. The brief for both product development and packaging design was to highlight a functional, retro feel that would appeal to urban professionals in Brooklyn and Manhattan.

Outcome: The Fitness Guru collection was released recently in New York West Elm stores.

above

The mood board seen here shows vintage images, old photographs, and other visuals that informed the designers as they developed a visual language for the products.

top

The packaging design is quirky and definitely functional. Sturdy cardboard tubes and minimalist paper wrappers protect the products, while the design highlights unusual hand-drawn shapes and rich colors that stand out nicely against the natural texture and background.

above

The designs used some "found" visuals that were cropped and manipulated to tie them into the retro feel. Likewise, imagery created specifically for the project was drawn in a style that worked with the overall brand.

CROPPING

Sometimes an image is perfect in its original form, but more often you will need to alter visual material to fit into a composition and balance with other elements like type, shape, and color. Cropping allows you to change the proportion or focal point of an image, use only part of an image, or repeat parts of an image. Designers often crop images when they want to create a more dynamic composition or frame content. They also use cropping to combine two or more visuals (for example when images are collaged together) or to distort the sense of scale. Once a visual has been cropped it can be used to signify movement or rhythm, to more effectively activate space, or to manipulate a viewer's sense of proportion and depth. When several images are cropped in the same way, the resulting series will invite comparisons. Cropping is most often done in programs like Adobe Photoshop, but images, textures, and patterns can also be cropped by hand with scissors or an X-Acto knife. It is definitely easier and faster to crop on the computer, but the act of cutting by hand will often produce different results and is especially helpful as you learn when and where to make cuts.

right

Cropping off the heads of the people in these photos allows viewers to feel a connection to the figures without seeing them as specific individuals. Having all the models wear similar T-shirts provides space to put the other necessary information.

Design: B12, Scottsdale, Arizona

Cut-outs: Images can be cropped or cut out using an outline of a shape or by following the compositional line created by other elements in the composition. Shapes and type can also be used as a mask for images to fit into. Cropping images and textures into a masked shape is a great way to create custom visuals and/or to effectively incorporate low-quality visuals into a composition.

TIPS FOR CROPPING IMAGES

- Always keep a version of the original image in case a different cropping is needed.

- When dealing with a central subject, tighter cropping tends to be more visually interesting.

- Avoid thinking exclusively in rectangles. Textures, patterns, and even photographic imagery can be cropped into shapes or large letterforms.

- Avoid cutting off subject matter at awkward points like the middle of a face or at the point an arm extends out of the composition unless the cropping is an intentional part of the design.

- Consider nontraditional cropping where an image is cut and rearranged or when two dissimilar images are paired together.

above

Imagery can be cropped so only part of the image will be seen in the design, or areas of an image can be cropped out with shape or letterform to help create a more unified composition. On this magazine page, several images are cropped to provide room for text and to break the regular rectangular proportions of the images.

Design: Cheah Wei Chun, CLANHOUSE, Singapore

LAYERING AND TRANSPARENCY

Most design software allows users to work in layers. Using this system, one element can be placed on top of another and moved independently or in conjunction with another linked element. Transparency settings within Adobe Photoshop and Illustrator also let users reduce the opacity of upper layers so layers beneath them can be seen. Blending modes in Adobe Photoshop and Illustrator allow the visual content on two or more layers to be combined using different pre-set effects. You can also "cut out" part of an image in Photoshop and place it on a layer above a different image to change the background to collage together several different types of visual material. These techniques offer users the ability to combine two or more visuals to create a new image or to juxtapose the content or ideas from the different images.

Layering, transparency, and blending modes are effective tools for creating custom visuals, but it's easy to go too far. Make sure layered images don't distract from other elements in the composition, and be on the lookout for instances where the image is obscured because of the layering or the use of blending modes. Images that have been combined with built-in software effects often look better on-screen than they do in print. If these effects produce muddy or ambiguous visuals, try reducing the number of effects or the amount of distortion used.

above

Transparency and layering can be physical as well as digital. In this example, the lettering on the windows provides a visual overlay for what is inside the building. If you are designing an interior space, consider the windows and lighting as well as the walls and any objects in the room.

Design: Marko Rašić & Vedrana Vrabec, Zagreb, Croatia

left

Layered blocks of color and type create depth in these photo-heavy editorial layouts. Notice how each image remains distinct even though layering is used.

Design: Cheah Wei Chun, CLANHOUSE, Singapore

COPYRIGHT AND LEGAL ISSUES

While you may not have a need to consider whether images or other visual material is copyrighted or is in the public domain because you don't make money on school projects, if you do plan to sell your work, even while you are still a student, copyright becomes an issue. Clearly once you begin to work as a professional designer (or to take on freelance side projects), it is essential to consider the ethical and legal implications of using visual material created by others in design projects. Then it is necessary to request written permission from the copyright holder to use his or her work, and there may also be a fee to pay for use of copyrighted imagery. The creator or originator of an image or piece of art usually retains the copyright for seventy years after the originator's death, but in certain cases that period may be extended and a family trust, a collector, or a museum may own the rights to an image indefinitely. In such cases, one has to check with the owner or trust to see if they will allow reproductions. Even if an organization allows reproductions, a fee is usually charged based on number of prints and the context in which the artwork will be used. When and where one can use copyrighted artwork and other visual material is a topic for more advanced study, but it is useful to remember that as soon as you start making work for hire, you will need to follow copyright law.

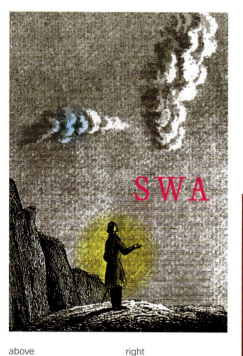

above

Using historic imagery is a way to avoid copyright issues. Adding color and or altering a found image can make it feel fresh and contemporary. If you decide to use found or historic images, check to make sure they can be reproduced without any copyright implications in the country where you are working.

Design: Aufuldish & Warinner, San Anselmo, California

right

When incorporating illustration or artwork into a design like the designers did on this book cover, it is important to get the artist's permission to use the work or to contact the collector or museum who owns the work so they can give you permission to reproduce it.

Design: Stephan Bundi, Boll, Switzerland

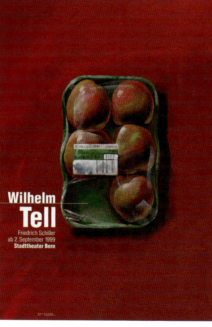

WHO OWNS IMAGES?

Fine art photography—the photographer holds the copyright.

Commercial photography (work for hire)—the client owns the image.

Fine art/personal illustration or artwork—the creator holds copyright.

Commissioned illustration—the company owns the copyright unless otherwise stipulated.

Design/photography/artwork created as part of one's job—the company owns the copyright.

Student work produced while studying—the creator owns the copyright, but some schools have stipulations allowing them to reproduce student artwork for publicity purposes.

CHAPTER IN REVIEW:
Do's and don'ts

1. Match the style of images used in a design to specific audience preferences or attributes and to the context where the final output will be seen. (p. 153)

2. Use images to catch a viewer's attention and garner visual interest. (p. 153)

3. Use the techniques described in the chapter to develop your own imagery if appropriate for the assignment. (p. 160)

4. Use formal variables such as lines and shapes to create more effective image-based compositions or unique visual identity systems. (p. 156)

5. Treat images carefully: avoid distorting proportions when scaling. (see Chapter 2, p. 74 and p. 174)

6. Work with image sizes and file formats appropriate to the specifications of the intended output (i.e., different for screen versus print applications). (p. 168 and page 171 for Inputting Artwork)

7. Prepare images for print or screen production. When going to print, images should be large enough that they are not pixelated or otherwise distorted (avoid imagery lower than 300 dpi for print projects). For screen and web-based outputs they should be small enough that they don't take too long to download. (p. 168 and p. 171 for Inputting Artwork)

8. Do not over-manipulate photographic images by using too many of the filters built into software programs. (p. 172)

9. Use copyright-free images or obtain image release when using images on client projects. (p. 176)

CHAPTER 7:
Layout and Arrangement

KEY TERMS AND CONCEPTS:

Columns are spatial containers used in layout. They are often created using the text box tool and may be linked together so content can flow from one column to another. (p. 201)

Flow lines (also called thresholds) are horizontal markers used for aligning and placing content. (see thresholds, p. 199)

Grids are structural systems for organizing content in graphic design projects. They include both horizontal and vertical thresholds or guidelines that indicate where text and images should be placed. (p. 197)

Guides (also called guidelines) are repositionable horizontal and vertical markers used for measuring and alignment purposes. Guides are visible on-screen but do not print unless the user specifically chooses to do so. (pp. 199 and 203)

Gutter is the space between two columns of text and/or between two pages in a book. The space between two pages is also called the fold or the spine. (p. 191)

Margins refer specifically to the space between the edge of the page and a marker or threshold where content begins. They can be set and repositioned in most design software programs. (p. 189)

Modular refers to a grid system with both horizontal and vertical divisions of space. Each module indicates alignment points where content can be placed. (p. 202)

Spreads are two pages that sit next to each other in a book or another design deliverable. (p. 195)

Thresholds (also called flow lines) are points or lines used by designers to align or place elements in a layout. Guides are often used to indicate thresholds. (p. 199)

IDENTIFYING AND TESTING EMPHASIS

Emphasis is always relative, and the degree to which one item stands out among others will depend on what is around it and its place in a composition. If an image is overpowered by large type, it will be less prominent, for example. On the other hand, a single, large image with small supporting type will carry most of the visual weight in a composition.

above

This layout achieves a good balance between type and image. The imagery makes the pages more interesting, but it doesn't disrupt a viewer's ability to easily read the text. Rules and color provide emphasis and an organizational structure for the text.

Design: THERE, Surry Hill, Australia

below

The heading stands out on this spread because it takes up an entire column and there is a heavy rule on top of the text. Without the rule, the text wouldn't appear to be grounded on the page and the heading would have less weight in the composition and would seem less important.

Design: THERE, Surry Hill, Australia

above

In these two layouts the image is the same size, but in the first layout the image has less visual weight because it is surrounded by large display text. The next layout includes more negative space around the image, and the negative space provides emphasis. The hierarchy in the second solution is clearer, and the information is clearly organized.

COMMON PROBLEMS WITH ARRANGEMENT

The diagrams below highlight common problems that occur when arranging content. Some issues have to do with arrangement. Others involve details like proximity and alignment. Look at each of the sample layouts and pick out the problem areas in the compositions and imagine what could have been done differently to produce better layouts.

above

Stepping type or image in a layout should be avoided because the content will appear scattered.

above

Visual tension created by elements in close proximity to each other or to a compositional edge should be avoided.

top right

This book spread is able to accommodate multiple alignment systems because they occur in different spatial areas. When working with more than one alignment system, make sure each piece of text is distinct and there is enough white space around the text so that there won't be visual confusion between different aspects of the text.

Design: Gerwin Schmidt, Munich, Germany

above

Listing dates and other supporting information may require a combination of two or more alignment systems.

EMPHASIZING WITH COLOR

When arranging elements in a composition, color and value are as important as scale and placement. As we discussed in Chapter 4 (p. 110), color affects hierarchy and provides emphasis. To develop effective layouts, you will need to pay special attention to the color of each element and make sure the colors you use support, rather than detract from, the overall hierarchy of the composition. The examples shown here illustrate how a composition changes when color is added to elements. Color isn't always beneficial. Some designs are more effective in black and white. To test whether color is improving or detracting from your own work, try eliminating color completely from a layout. Then step back and evaluate the result. Has the emphasis changed? Is the composition more or less engaging? If the color you have in your layout doesn't improve the design, review the information on different methods for choosing color palettes from Chapter 4 or use only black and white.

above

The less color present in a composition, the more noticeable individual hues will be.

above

When color is added to text, it sets it apart. Make sure color is enhancing, and not detracting from, the overall hierarchy when it is used on text.

above

Since warm colors stand out against cooler tones, adding a warm color to the foreground can provide emphasis. This technique can also be used to create a sense of depth on a flat page.

above

Even when no color is present, value can change the hierarchy of a composition.

above and left

Color helps provide emphasis and differentiate each section of this website and app. Navigation text and headings remain in the same place on each page. Consistent placement of elements like text and imagery is a good way to establish continuity between pages or items in a series.

Design: Project Projects, New York

right

We might commonly think of color helping to denote emphasis in a particular area of a composition, but color can also differentiate particular sections or pages in a multipage document. This example shows how a single, full-color page breaks up the content and stands out against the pages with more imagery on the right and left.

Design: THERE, Surry Hill, Australia

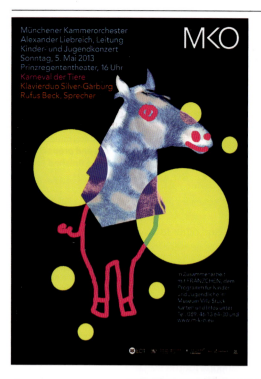

Margins provide consistency on applications as well as in print.

Design: Lotta Nieminen, New York

This poster uses consistent margins on all sides. This is a good way of making the content feel framed within a particular space.

Design: Gerwin Schmidt, Munich, Germany

In this example, tighter margins allow more content to be placed on the pages.

Here is an example with more generous margins. The layout feels open and airy, and the content is given room to breathe, but this system will also result in the need for more pages.

There are numerous ways of incorporating text and imagery within the same spread. Whether imagery should conform to the edges of the margins, break the margins and bleed over all the edges, or cross over the gutter depends on the content and the stylistic tone of the piece. Here the overall margins are generous, but the secondary margins between the edge of the white area and the text are much tighter.

The margins provide a frame for the image in this example. On the right side of the spread, the text also stays within the thresholds provided by the margins. Two columns allow for easy reading, and the heading at the top gives the viewer immediate information about the content.

Chapter 7 / Layout and Arrangement

GUTTERS

The gutter is the space between pages or columns of text. Gutters are important for two reasons: When they occur between columns in either print or screen-based designs, they visually mark the break between sections of text and give the eye a chance to rest. They also occur in the space between pages. Here it is called the fold or the spine, and this space also disrupts the flow of content. To effectively design book spreads, you will need to mitigate the disruption that is caused by the spine. Avoid overly narrow gutters because the columns of text will seem crowded. However, columns need to feel visually connected to each other. If columns are too far apart, a viewer may not continue to read from one to the next.

Some bindings don't allow pages to open flat, and the fold may obscure part of the page. To solve this problem you should avoid extending content beyond the interior margins on each side of the fold. Depending on the overall size of the page and the binding you are working with, it might be necessary to add extra space to the interior margins. This will ensure content isn't lost in the gutter/fold and will make it easier to flow text and images onto densely packed pages.

gutter

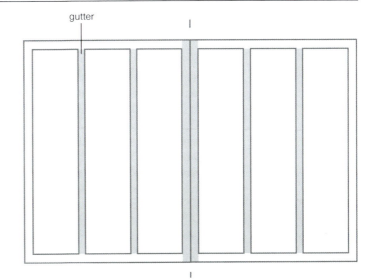

above

The gutter refers to the fold between each side of the spread or the space between two columns of text.

left

These spreads highlight different ways of dealing with the gutter in a multipage document. In the top spread the image on the left is centered on the page, while the one on the right is bled to fill the entire page running over the gutter. The lower spread staggers the columns of text providing a very open-looking layout. The placement of the left-hand column next to the gutter visually connects the text to the right-hand page.

Design: Gerwin Schmidt, Munich, Germany

above

In this example, the image crosses over the gutter, connecting the two pages in the spread. Text is set in columns which also have their own gutters.

LIMITS AND FLEXIBILITY

Sometimes grids get a bad reputation because people think they are too structured or stifle creativity. In fact, the opposite is true. Grids are used to produce both highly structured and extremely experimental work. The grid itself isn't limiting; limits come from how you decide to use the grid. At first it is hard not to slavishly adhere to the system you have created. It's easy to get wrapped up in following the rules, and your first layouts produced may seem a bit stilted. Don't worry; the more you work with grids, the easier it gets.

Grids can be as flexible as you need them to be. Remember, you are in charge. You can always go back and revise or re-create your grid. And you can break the "rules" set up by the structure of grid models to produce better layouts. Think of a grid as a tool rather than as a set of absolutes.

below

All these packages for children's clay are designed using the same grid. This creates consistency when packages of different colored clays are seen together. Notice how the grid lines provide information about where to space the content so it will appear correctly on each side of the package.

Design: Marko Rašić & Vedrana Vrabec, Zagreb, Croatia

SYMMETRY VERSUS ASYMMETRY

When you begin to develop a grid you will have to decide whether to use a symmetrical or asymmetrical system. Grid modules or alignment points mirror each other in symmetrical grids. In asymmetrical grids, a quadrant appears in different positions on each side of the spread or page. Asymmetrical grids are used on single-page formats such as posters and websites. Keep in mind that the layouts of individual spreads aren't necessarily symmetrical, even when a symmetrical grid has been used.

Asymmetrical grids (below bottom) work well if content will vary considerably from one side of the spread to the other or if you want certain areas of the page to be reserved for particular content (like images). *Asymmetrical* grids are also a mainstay in web design where single pages are seen one after another rather than two at a time, like in books or magazines.

above

Symmetrical grids (in the top spread) are used for content-heavy, multipage documents such as books or magazines. If you want both pages in a spread to have the same margins and you want to instill a sense of continuity in the document, then a symmetrical grid will probably work best.

TYPES OF GRIDS

Grids can be as simple or complex as you need them to be. Sometimes a grid consists of only a couple of guidelines or flow lines. More fully developed grids are produced using a number of horizontal and vertical thresholds or rectangles indicating where to place headings, body text, and even page numbers. Designers also produce experimental grids. These can be based on lines, objects, or any element that inspires the designer. Once you become comfortable working with simple grids, try developing a more experimental grid and applying the grid to a range of project types. You may find you are more comfortable working with common forms of grids, or you might discover a new talent and decide to develop unusual grids for each project. The next section describes several common types of grids. But you don't necessarily have to use one of these systems. Grids can be based on measurements of a typeface or the size of a single page or even a shape or image.

below

This website uses grid systems for accommodating different types of and sizes of text and image content. When more content needs to be on a page, the imagery is smaller, but not so small that it seems cluttered. When working with multiple grids in the same piece, try to develop alignment points that are consistent between each type of pages.

Design: THERE, Surry Hill, Australia

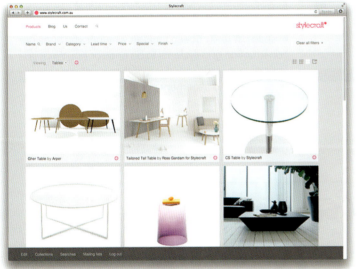

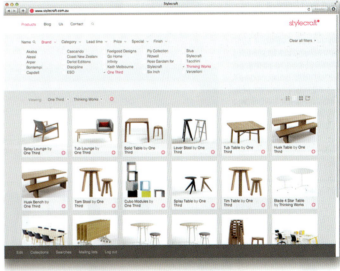

WIREFRAMES

Wireframes are used in screen-based designs and are similar to grids. They are structural models showing functionality, navigation, and separate areas for content on websites and applications. Like other types of grids, wireframe are used to indicate hierarchy and where to place text and image elements on a page or a series of pages.

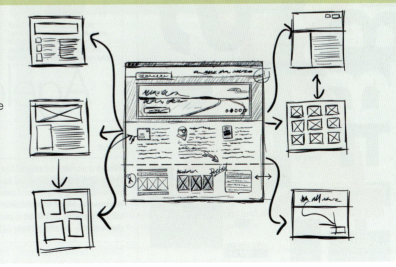

After you have decided on the overall page size and set the margins, you will need to consider the width of individual columns. If columns are too narrow, the text won't flow correctly and large spaces will occur either on the right edge of the column (in flush left orientated situations, p. 128) or rivers will appear in the text (in justified text, p. 129). If the columns are too wide, the length of each line of type will be long, making it difficult for the viewer to follow along from one column to the next.

Adding horizontal axis lines or flow lines to a column grid will extend the grid's function. This is a good option when body text needs to begin at different places because of chapters or section starts. More thresholds are also helpful when laying out pages with diverse visual elements.

MODULAR

Modular grids (see p. 204) use horizontal and vertical alignment markers to divide space into equally sized quadrants or cells. Gutters between the modules ensure there is space between visual elements and text. Depending on their size, individual cells can be used to hold chunks of text and imagery, or several cells can be combined to create larger spatial zones. Module grids are a good choice when both horizontal and vertical alignment points are needed and in cases where the visual material is quite varied and includes text, imagery, marginalia, and call-outs. The size of the individual cells has a significant impact on the effectiveness of the overall grid. If the modules are too small, there will be so many options for alignment that the practical purpose of the grid will be obscured. If modules are too large, there may not be enough areas indicated for placement. Work will be slow, and the resulting layout may lack continuity.

above

Just because you are working with a three-column grid doesn't mean you need to have three columns of text on each page. This grid is flexible enough to accommodate both type- and image-heavy layouts. When there is more imagery, one or two columns of text are used rather than three per page.

Design: Cheah Wei Chun, CLANHOUSE, Singapore

right

A grid where modules touch the edge of the page can be confusing to work with because it can seem like content should be placed next to the edge.

COMBINING GRID SYSTEMS

What type of grid is best for a project will vary depending on the requirements of the assignment and your own working process. Sometimes a simple constructional grid will produce the most successful layout, but in other situations it might be best to customize one of the systems described here or to create an entirely new structure. The same grid can produce very different looking layouts. In some cases, the shape and location of cells will clearly indicate what content should be placed within them, but the designer always reserves the right to break the grid with call-outs, imagery, or other elements.

Try working with a variety of grids and pay attention to which yields the best results. Experimentation is key.

USING DESIGN SOFTWARE TO CREATE GRIDS

Grids are used most often in page layout software like InDesign, but you may develop a grid in any design software program. As stated previously, you should make sketches of the composition before laying out the content in design software.

Once you start working in the software it is best to use the document setup window to specify page size, margin size, and column width (if applicable). When working in Adobe Photoshop or Illustrator, you can create a separate layer for the grid or simply work with guides, turning them on and off as needed. In InDesign, grids are typically created on the master page(s) and then applied to other pages in the layout. You may need to try several grid systems before arriving at one that produces attractive results. The best way to tell whether a grid is successful is to test it by laying out sample pages. If it feels too constrained or doesn't have enough alignment points to indicate where content should be placed, go back and revise the grid.

CONSIDERATIONS BEFORE CREATING A GRID

- Evaluate where the content/information will be seen, i.e., is it a website, poster, or book?

- Are multiple columns needed? If so, consider using a module or column grid.

- Will the content work better with a looser grid system or a tighter one? If speed is a concern and the document has a lot of pages, it will probably be faster to use a more structured grid.

- Does it make sense to base the grid on an aspect of the content or some proportion otherwise derived from the content? For example, a book about trees might use the proportion derived from a leaf as the basis for a grid.

- Are existing grid systems such as the ones previously described appropriate to use on the project? If not, consider creating a non-standard or unusual grid.

EXERCISE:
Creating a grid

In this exercise you will learn to develop a grid for a multipage document or a website. You can use one of the grid systems described in this chapter, or you can create your own format for the grid. If your grid is difficult to work with, ask an instructor for help or start with a grid more like the ones discussed in this chapter.

1. Decide which type of grid will be most appropriate for the content and the format you are working with. For example, should it be symmetrical or asymmetrical? Is it best to work with a constructional, columnar, or modular format?

2. Determine and set page or format size.

3. Evaluate whether the content will be best suited to a single- or multi-column grid structure.

4. Define the outer edges of the page using margins and set up multiple columns (if applicable).

5. If you are working with a multi-column grid, take the time to test different column widths and margin spacing with samples of text.

6. Position main alignment thresholds using guides. Then add additional thresholds if needed.

7. Make revisions if needed and apply the grid structure to master pages (InDesign) or on a separate layer (Photoshop and Illustrator).

8. Begin laying out text and image content using the grid system. If you struggle with some spreads or content areas/frames, move on to others and come back to the difficult ones later.

9. Show your layouts to a fellow classmate or an instructor. Ask for feedback and revise your layouts based on their suggestions.

10. Once a project is finished, assess whether the grid made laying out content easier or faster. If not, examine what went wrong and what you would do differently the next time you work with a grid.

below

This book uses a simple one-column grid for pages that are text heavy and those that are image dominant. The margins are generous, and the page numbers are aligned at the top right of the text block rather than at the bottom.

Design: Esen Karol, Istanbul, Turkey

CHAPTER IN REVIEW:
Do's and don'ts

1. Explore a variety of systems for arrangement while maintaining hierarchy. (pp. 180–182)

2. Review the first steps in layout before placing visuals in the composition. (p. 181)

3. Make sure your layouts are using emphasis to maintain and enhance visual hierarchy. (p. 152 and see p. 122 for more information on hierarchy)

4. Set margins and decide on a page size/format before adding image and text to a composition. (p. 189)

5. Avoid placing text or imagery too close to the edge of a page unless it is supposed to bleed off the edge. (pp. 189–190)

6. Design pages as spreads rather than individually when working on multipage documents. (p. 195)

7. Use alignment, grids, and other layout strategies to maintain continuity between pages when working in spreads or other multipage documents like apps and websites. (p. 197)

8. Experiment with grid systems and choose one that will accommodate the content and the format of the final design. (p. 203)

9. If your grid makes laying out content difficult, revise it. (p. 198)

10. Before creating a grid on the computer, review the section that describes how to create a grid using design software. (p. 203)

Chapter 8 / Context and Production

CHAPTER 8:
Context and Production

KEY TERMS AND CONCEPTS:

Binding is to physically collect and assemble pages into a book, brochure, or another multipage or folded form. (p. 216)

Backing up refers to copying or archiving computer files and is used to prevent data loss in the event of unforeseen problems with computers and other storage devices. (p. 228)

Comp is a shortened version of the word "comprehensive." The term refers to stages in the design process where layouts of proposed solutions are shown to clients or to an instructor. Comps can be made using a variety of media, and on professional projects they are often shown to clients before starting final production of a design. (p. 210)

Duplex printing is another word for double-sided printing. (p. 211)

Embossing/debossing is a process used to create raised or recessed images or other visuals on paper or another substrate. (p. 212)

Ink-jet printing sprays wet ink onto specially coated papers to produce intensely colored prints and is ideal for large-format pieces like signage and banners and for photography. (p. 211)

Laser printing adheres ink made of dry pigments to paper using heat. It is fast and inexpensive, and these printers may print only black and white or both color and black and white. (p. 211)

Mounting refers to a process where one substrate is fixed to another. In graphic design projects, paper printouts or drawings are usually pasted on to board or Foamcore (p. 217) before being presented. (p. 224)

Offset printing is a technique where the inked image is transferred from a metal plate to a rubber blanket and then to the paper. Offset printing is typically used for projects requiring more than 2,000 copies and/or for projects requiring very high-quality prints. (p. 212)

Photo mock up is a way of digitally showing a final design in a physical context and is a common way of presenting work for critique. For example, a poster might be shown on a bus stop, and the design of a sign would be added to an image of the exterior of a building. (p. 210)

Pixilation occurs when an image is of low quality or has been enlarged to the point where it becomes blurry or individual pixels are visible. Photographs, scans and other bitmap images are subject to pixilation. (p. 168)

Proofing is the testing of a print or a design before a piece goes to final production. For example, one will proof or test colors several times before printing a large poster or multipage project like a book. (p. 214)

Resolution refers to the quality or clarity of a raster-based (see p. 168) digital image such as a photograph or scan. Generally, the higher the resolution the greater the clarity/quality of the image will be. (p. 214)

Save-as is a command in the file menu of most design software that allows users copy the current document and save a new version of it in a different location or with a different name. (p. 228)

Scoring (also called creasing) compresses the paper along a fold line, making folding easier and neater. Scoring may be done with a bone fold (p. 217) or another sharp instrument. (p. 221)

Trimming flush is trimming to the edge of the composition. If something is trimmed flush, it has no border. (p. 224)

PRODUCTION BASICS

Production and finishing transform ideas and software files into finished design projects. First-year students rarely need to know how to send files to a commercial printer, nor are they expected to understand the nuances of digital and on-screen production. But you will need to create a finished version of your designs to show in a critique and to put in your portfolio. It is helpful to familiarize yourself with the materials used to produce two- and three-dimensional design projects. In this section we will learn about types of printing, common binding and finishing methods, and the tools needed to create mock-ups of finished design projects. If you are working exclusively on interactive or screen-based assignments, learning about print production may not be necessary, and you may jump ahead to the section on Presentation and Feedback on page 225.

THE COMP

In graphic design and advertising, mock-ups of design layouts are called comps. The term is an abbreviation for comprehensive which is a visual layout of a design solution shown either in digital form or as a two or three-dimensional mock-up. In professional practice, comps are shown to clients before the final version of the design goes into production. The placement of text and imagery is indicated, as are colors and other visual choices. A comp can be accepted as is, or the client may ask the designer to make further revisions before production begins.

Design students use comps differently than professionals. Producing a comp is usually the last thing students do before completing their assignment. Comps are shown in the same format as the final version of the project will be seen. For example, books and magazine spreads are printed, packaging is constructed in a three-dimensional form, and the designs for websites and apps are shown on-screen. For complicated and oversized designs, it is usually acceptable to show a digital mock-up where the layout of the design is added to a photograph of an actual environment or shown using three-dimensional digital rendering. Check with your instructor before producing comps. Your instructor will tell you what is considered acceptable for each assignment.

above

This promotions piece uses details like red cord, a deep-blue paper folder, and a simple minimalistic design. Production is part of your designs, so try using unusual materials and high-quality papers to enhance your work.

Design: Anagrama, Nuevo Leon, Mexico

right

Both students and professional designers can use comps to show what final work will look like when it is finished. When showing work on-screen, it is often helpful to mock up the design on an actual screen, as was done here for this project. This way the viewer or client can imagine actually using the application.

Design: This is Folly, Minneapolis, Minnesota

TYPES OF PRINTING

Most design projects are printed using one of two methods. The first is digital printing, and this system includes both inkjet and laser printing. The second is offset lithography. Typically student projects are printed using digital printing, whereas professional projects are more often printed using offset lithography. Considerations such as cost, quantity, and quality will determine which type of printing is best to use.

DIGITAL PRINTING

Digital printing includes both laser and ink-jet printing. These systems are cost effective for home and school setups. When working on professional projects, designers use digital printing to proof work, for large-format projects, and for projects requiring fewer than 2,000 copies. Both copy centers and professional print shops usually offer digital services. Digital printing is the most common form of printing used by students to produce design projects for classes and their portfolios.

Ink-jet printing

Ink-jet printers spray wet ink onto specially coated papers to produce intensely colored prints. This type of printing is ideal for large-format pieces like signage and banners and for photography. Ink-jet printing is relatively slow, so this isn't a good choice when you need multiple copies of the same design. Since colors are bright and fairly true, ink-jet printing works well for posters and image-dominant work.

Laser printing

Laser printers adhere ink made of dry pigments to paper using heat. Laser printing is fast and inexpensive and is available in either black and white or color. Multiple copies can be printed in less than a minute. Because laser printers only take one or two sizes of paper (the most common being 8.5 × 11 inches and 11 × 17 inches in the United States) they don't work well for large-format projects. Colors have a tendency to be more muted and darker than what you see on screen. To match the colors on your screen, you may need to run tests and make color adjustments. Better quality laser printers offer duplexing (double-sided) functions and booklet printing. They are a good option when working on multipage projects.

top

These canister labels were professionally printed, but if you were going to create a three-dimensional comp or example of a similar project, it would be important to test the colors because layering imagery often looks different on-screen than it does in print.

Design: Sonsoles Llorens, Barcelona, Spain

above

This packaging design was printed on a laser printer using semi-gloss paper. The student then folded the paper to make it into the shape and size of an actual Tetra-pak®. Laser printing works well for comps and student projects, and if you are careful when you put pieces together, they can look like they were professionally produced.

Design: Idalea Cinquemani, New York

above

Embossing/debossing is a printing process where a special plate is used to create raised or recessed images or other visuals on paper or another substrate. Specialty finishes often cost more, but as you can see from this example, the debossing of the bees and lines gives dimension to the page.

Design: Goetz Gramlich, Heidelberg, Germany

OFFSET LITHOGRAPHY

Most professional design projects are printed using offset lithography (also called offset printing) because it cost-effectively produces large quantities of high-quality prints. To print using this system, the file of the final layout of a design is separated into the colors cyan, magenta, yellow, and black (CMYK, see p. 88). The metal plates are coated with light-sensitive material in the areas where each color is present in the layout and then run through the printer. Because of the time it takes to separate designs into different plates, this type of printing is usually done on jobs requiring more than 2,000 copies. Offset lithography is too expensive for most school projects.

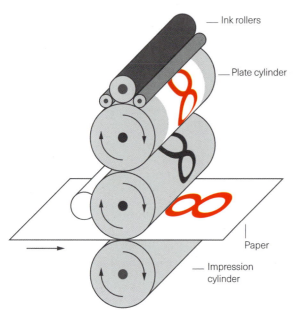

— Ink rollers

— Plate cylinder

Paper

— Impression cylinder

left

This diagram shows the offset printing process. The content of a layout is transfered onto metal printing plates. Ink rollers transfer ink onto the plate cylinder which then transfers the image onto a rubber blanket and then onto the paper or the printing surface.

above

This piece is printed with fully saturated colors and offset lithography. Offset lithography provides more options for custom color and finishes than laser or ink-jet printing and is the best option if you want to use metallic or fluorescent inks.

Design: Anagrama, Nuevo Leon, Mexico

Background

When the designers at Cast Iron Design began work on re-branding Roger the Barber, Roger had already been cutting hair for thirty-three years. Unlike in most salons, Roger handles every session himself, one person at a time. Roger is known for his meticulous attention to detail and his modern take on classic styles and for his endless enthusiasm.

Designing for digital and physical outputs

Roger serves a very specific clientele and has certain requirements his clients must be aware of before booking a cut. When Cast Iron Designers worked on Roger's website, they designed a menu to provide a brief overview of services offered while allowing return customers to quickly book an appointment. They integrated a booking system that Roger can easily manage using his iPad. Both the website and iPad booking system use the same visuals and scrolling format.

Printing and production

Roger needed a way to direct walk-in customers to his website in order to book an appointment. The designers' solution was to create a small, concise, digitally printed card. The small size (1.5 × 2.75 inches) allowed them to nearly double the number of cards on a 12 × 18 inch press sheet (in comparison to a standard 2 × 3.5 inch business card), reducing paper and printing costs. For the paper the designers specified Mohawk's *Inxwell Vellum*, a digital ready stock with a subtle texture that worked well for the small size of the card.

They specified the aforementioned stock for two different jobs using offset printing, which they ran simultaneously, saving costs for both clients and minimizing their trips to the printer for quality checks.

IMAGE RESOLUTION AND PRINTING

The image size and resolution needed for a project will depend on the specifications of the final output and where it will be seen. For example, the resolution required for a billboard will be different from what is needed for a website, an annual report, or a book. Large-format projects require bigger images than small projects. Screen resolution is 72 dpi, and this is the size used on screen-based projects (for more on image resolution and images, see p. 168). Most print production projects require 300 dpi images at 100 percent of their intended size. If you are using a commercial printer or a copy center, it is a good idea to see if they have any special requirements. Different printers may have their own set of specifications.

Both offset lithography and digital printing use the CMYK color system, so unless otherwise specified, imagery should be delivered in this spectrum and in a loss-less format like TIFF (tagged image file format) or EPS (encapsulated post script). Vector-based images like line art, illustrations, and logotypes are usually created in a software program like Adobe Illustrator. They are infinitely scalable, and the output device will control their size. Vector files should be saved in the EPS or PDF format for optimal results. In Photoshop, it is preferable to save imagery in the TIFF format unless a transparent background is required. In that case, it is acceptable to save an image as a Photoshop PSD file, but all layers except the transparent background should be merged. Final versions of imagery should be saved in the correct format (EPS, TIFF or PSD) and flattened (unless the image has a transparent background) before they are placed into layout programs like InDesign.

Printing PDFs

PDF files are usually printed using Adobe Acrobat instead of the software where the original file was produced. They offer several advantages. PDFs are particularly useful if you are going to hand off your files to a print center or lab because they provide a good working proof of what your file will look like when it has been printed. They also contain font information so you won't have to install non-system-standard fonts on the computer you print from. Most design software allows you to save the files as PDFs. The color profiles are sometimes different when printing from Acrobat than from other programs. Check with the service provider or lab technician if exact color matching is important.

above

The Minneapolis-based design studio This is Folly developed the brand identity and collateral for MIX, the city's new Idea eXchange sponsored by the Minneapolis Downtown Council. The branding materials for MIX were produced both digitally and in print, so the designers had to prepare their files with different resolutions (or dpi), depending on which piece they producing.

Design: This is Folly, Minneapolis, Minnesota

PACKAGING FILES IN INDESIGN

Images and fonts are not embedded in InDesign files. They are linked. When you need to move a file from one computer to another, you need to make sure to move the linked images and fonts as well as the InDesign file. The best way to move InDesign files to another computer is to package the file. Packaging will collect the InDesign layout file, and all the images, graphics, and fonts used into a new folder. This folder of packaged files will include separate subfolders for linked graphics and fonts. By packaging InDesign files you can easily move working files to another computer, and this system also ensures all components of a file are properly organized and linked for printing.

SAVING PDF'S

From Illustrator = File <save as>

From Photoshop = File <save as>

From Microsoft Word = File <save as>

From InDesign = File <Adobe PDF Presets> Then choose the quality you want

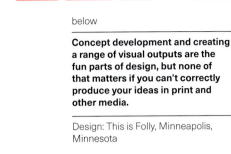

The blocky M was inspired by the solid flour mills and warehouses in Minneapolis, the I represents people and ideas, and the x represents the intersecting of ideas to create something new.

Design: This is Folly, Minneapolis, Minnesota

below

Concept development and creating a range of visual outputs are the fun parts of design, but none of that matters if you can't correctly produce your ideas in print and other media.

Design: This is Folly, Minneapolis, Minnesota

PRINTING CHECKLIST

Use the following checklist to ensure your files are ready to print.

- Decide which type of printer will be used and check to see if there are any specifications stipulated by the print center or lab.

- Check to see whether all files are properly linked (only applies to layout programs such as InDesign, Illustrator, and Quark Express).

- If working with multiple layers, flatten before printing. But save an editable version in case you want to go back and make changes.

- Check to see that the color profiles in the design software match the ones used by the printer. (This isn't always possible, but it is particularly important with ink-jet printers.)

- Make sure imagery is not pixelated, stretched, or otherwise distorted.

- Check whether all fonts are properly installed on the computer you are printing from (not applicable if printing from PDF).

- Choose single- or double-sided printing, depending on the project requirements.

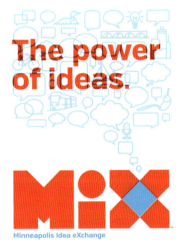

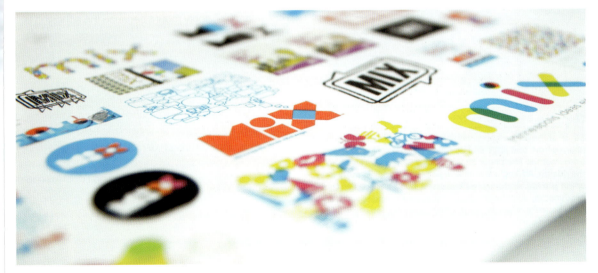

left

This image shows the wide range of visual explorations the designers worked on before deciding on the geometric red and blue text. Even if your favorite solution isn't chosen for production, you should save your work and keep it as reference for future projects.

Design: This is Folly, Minneapolis, Minnesota

BINDING

Binding uses glue, thread/string, or wire and plastic combs/spirals to permanently hold multiple pages together. Each binding technique produces a unique visual appearance, and some are easier to do by hand than others. Choosing an appropriate binding for course projects should be done with the help of an instructor.

below
_____

Specialty bindings include boxes, sleeves, and ties. This example shows how custom finishes and bindings transform a series of books or brochures into a single product.

Design: Sonsoles Llorens, Barcelona, Spain

Perfect binding

Perfect binding (also known as adhesive binding) is widely used by the publishing industry. Most paperback books and magazines are bound using this method. Pages of the same size are stacked together and adhesive is applied to the edge of the pages along one side. Books bound using this method have a uniform rectangular appearance. They open flat or nearly flat. One limitation to this system is the number of pages needed to achieve successful adhesion. Depending on the weight of the paper, one needs at least twenty sheets of paper for perfect binding. If too few pages are used or if the glue fails to properly adhere to the spine, individual pages can come loose from the sequence. Normally, a heavy-weight paper or board is used to create a sturdy cover for perfect bound books.

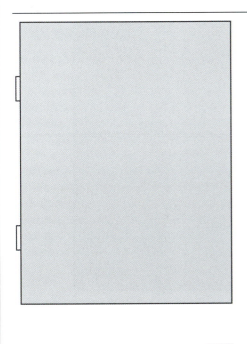

Saddle stitch

In saddle stitching both sides of a spread are printed on the same piece of paper. All the pages are gathered together and folded in half. One or more staples are placed along the fold line and through the pages. The staples are closed in the center spread. Some staplers have an extra-long arm to allow you to staple through wider sheets of paper. If a long-armed stapler isn't available you can still use the saddle stitch method to produce one or two books at a time. Use a needle, an awl, or even one of the legs of staple to poke through each individual sheet at the points where the staples will go through the paper (measuring may be necessary). Then manually thread the staple through and press the ends closed with a pen cap or coin. Manual saddle stitching is inefficient, but it is effective when producing a single bound object.

above

This brochure uses saddle stitch binding. The binding allows the brochure to open flat and the full color images to be displayed well. Since it can be done cheaply and by hand with long-arm staplers, saddle stitch binding is a suitable option for student projects.

Design: THERE, Surry Hill, Australia

Four-page simple fold

A single fold is made in the middle of a sheet of paper. This folding structure produces four panels.

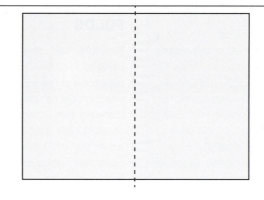
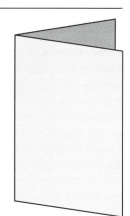

Four-page short fold

The short fold is a variation on the simple fold. Here, the placement of the fold is asymmetrical, and it results in two larger and two smaller panels.

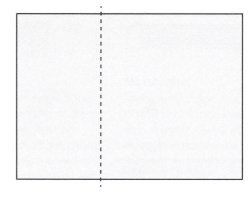
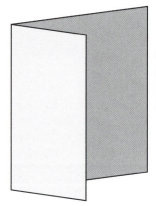

Accordion fold

To create an accordion fold, paper is folded at least two times. Each of the folds bends in the opposite direction as the previous one. If the paper is folded at regular intervals the panels will be of equal size, but if the distance between the folds varies, pages will have the same vertical size but a different horizontal size.

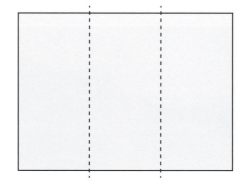
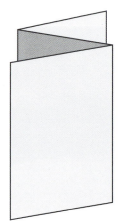

Barrel fold

One or two sides of the paper are folded so the outer edges of the panel are folded in towards the center. Flaps on the inside can be used as panels for content.

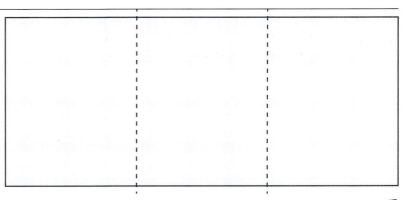

French fold

The sheet of paper is folded first horizontally and then vertically. When the piece is fully folded, it has a smaller trim size but it can be fully opened to reveal a large panel the full size of the sheet.

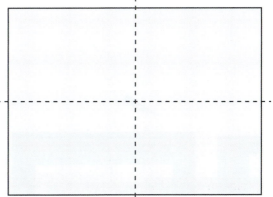

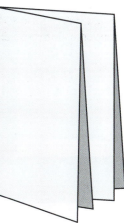

DESIGN AS A WORKING PROCESS

Design is both a creative and a practical process. As a design student, you will learn different ways to approach visual problems and how to develop concepts. You will also learn to use relevant software and how to produce your projects for print and screen-based outputs. Professional designers create great concepts and visuals, but they also understand the practical aspects of project management. These skills include time management, file naming, saving and backing up work, and binding and finishing practices like those detailed in the previous section. In school, you can use class assignments to learn these skills. Developing good working habits will make you a better student and prepare you to work in a professional setting.

INCREMENTAL GOALS AND TIME ALLOTMENT

Students often have trouble estimating how long it will take to complete their projects. This is normal, and instructors may break down assignments into specific tasks with targeted completion dates to help you manage each part of the project. If you have a busy schedule it can be tempting to wait until the last minute or several hours before a due date to work on your assignment. Unfortunately, procrastination rarely yields positive results. Designs produced at the last minute look rushed and incomplete. Using an assignment book or reminders on your phone can help you keep track of due dates and avoid the last-minute rush. You may be given a handout outlining expectations for the project, or your instructor may verbally explain the requirements. As your instructor reviews the assignment, take notes and write down when specific parts of the project are due. Typically, larger projects will follow the design process outlined in Chapter 2. Shorter exercises may focus on specific steps of the design process and are completed more quickly than projects using the entire design process. Regardless of whether you are working on an exercise or a larger project, it is always best to start work as soon as possible. If you finish tasks ahead of time you can always go back and revise your work once or twice before showing it to the class.

DESIGN IN ACTION:
Christmas Gifts by Marko Rašić & Vedrana Vrabec (Studio Rašić), Zagreb, Croatia

Every year, Studio Rasic gives a Christmas present to its partners and some of the people the designers work with. They create a series of bottles of wine inspired by their philosophy, projects, and clients and they produce the labels themselves.

below

The wine label becomes a Christmas playground for these designers. This variety is called Handmade—and was inspired by the idea that every "Handmade" wine is unique and handmade, just like it says on the label.

right

Music Wines: Each wine bottle sings its own song—Feeling Good, Summertime, Fly Like an Eagle—and a few Christmas songs as well—Little Drummer Boy, Happy Xmas... For each client the designers chose one song that somehow connects them to a common event, success, failure, laughter, or something personal.

below

Medicine wine: "Medicine wine" is wine that Marko and Vedrana send to their clients from pharmaceutical industry or to clients and friends who use too much of a specific medication. Labels look the same as original packaging for medications that are recognizable in Croatia.

Conclusion

CONCLUSION

As we have learned, design is both a conceptual and a practical process. It occurs when great ideas are visualized using type, images, and other materials. The content covered in this book is just the beginning of your education as a designer. As you move on to more advanced classes, you will acquire new skills and explore different ways of delivering content to users.

Learning is a lifelong process. Try to be a sponge and absorb the visual world around you. Soon you will begin to see the world through the eyes of a designer. Badly kerned letters will annoy you, the colors in the environment will ask to be used in design projects, and you will start seeing textures and patterns as raw material rather than as a backdrop. As you continue to hone your design skills, you will join a community of people who are passionately committed to solving practical problems and exploring new visual territory. Design is more than just a job; it is a way of life.

Welcome to the world of design!

GLOSSARY

Active or activating refers to literal or implied movement in design. Activating part of a design or a composition means to consider all areas of the page or live area and to place elements so the space is balanced and hierarchy is maintained. An *active* design is generally considered better than one that is static.

Abstraction or abstract images exist with some degree of independence from the natural world and strict representation. An abstraction of a person's face might no longer look like the model who posed for the photograph, for example.

Additive color closely mimics how light stimulates the eye; this system is used in screen design.

Analog refers to art or design processes that originate with the human hand. Painting on canvas and sculpting clay are analog processes.

Assets are items such as text, imagery, textures, and other visual elements that will be used in a design project. Assets may be given to you as part of an assignment, or you may have to find or create your own assets.

Black (when used to describe a typeface) refers to a heavy-weight version of a typeface and is normally even heavier than *bold*.

Bleed is a predetermined margin outside the trim area of a composition and is a term used in commercial printing. When a document is printed, the ink extends out to the edge of the bleed. Then the bleed area is trimmed off. When using this system, text and imagery will touch the edge of the page.

Brightness refers to the relative degree of lightness or darkness of a color.

Body copy (also called body text or running text) refers to multiple lines of text set together and/or text that is set in paragraph format.

Brainstorming uses lists, diagrams, and sketches as an activity to develop creative solutions.

Color is perceived by the eye when light reflects off different surfaces. The length and quality of the light being reflected produces a variety of types and intensity of color.

Color palette is a limited set of colors that have been chosen for use in composition or set of design deliverables. Color palettes often include dominant tones, which are used frequently or for more important content, as well as subordinate or accent colors, which are used more sparingly.

Color theory is the study of how hues relate to each other and affect a viewer's perceptions.

Columns are spatial containers used in layout. Columns are often created using the text box tool and may link together so content can flow from one column to another.

Composition or compositional space is the area where layout or design occurs.

Comp is a shortened version of the word comprehensive. The term refers to stages in the design process where layouts of proposed solutions are shown to clients or to an instructor. Comps can be made using a variety of media, and on professional projects they are often shown to clients before final production of a design is started.

Concept is the idea behind a design.

Contrast occurs when two things are different from each other. Scale, color, and style can all produce contrast.

Cool colors have underlying tones of blue.

Copyright is a legal right that gives the originator of an artwork or a design exclusive rights to use or distribute the work within a geographic region and for a given amount of time. Copyright law varies depending on the laws of a particular country.

Cropping is removal of parts of an image or other element to improve the framing of a single element or an overall composition.

Design process is a repeatable series of actions used to develop design projects. The design process begins with the brief and ends with production or dissemination to the viewer or user.

Digital art and design uses technology in its production or distribution. For example, a digital drawing can be created directly with a computer stylus, while a digital print may have originally been created by hand but a computer-based technique is used to reproduce it.

Display type (also called display text) is larger type typically used for headlines or titles. Text type can also be used as display if the letterforms are clearly visible when they are enlarged. Display type may require extra kerning to ensure letters appear evenly spaced.

DPI (dots per inch) is a measurement of the density of pixels or dots in given area and is used in computer-generated graphics.

Drop-down or flyaway menus exist in most design software. They are not seen until the user clicks on them, and then they offer secondary options for changing the attributes of an element or file. Once the user has made his/her choice, they revert back to the inactive state.

Duotone was traditionally defined as half-tone reproduction of an image using black plus another color. Today, design software allows you to create duotones for both print and screen-based designs, and they can include any two colors.

Duplex printing is another word for double-sided printing.

Element is an item such as a line, type, or image that exists within a composition. (Also see *form* and *figure*.)

Figure is another word for form. The front or foreground of a composition is made up of elements, or forms. Behind the forms is the ground, background, or negative space. (Also see *form* and *element*.)

Flow lines (also called thresholds) are horizontal markers used for aligning and placing content.

Form refers to any element in a design. Images, type, and even dots or lines are all form. (Also see *figure* and *element*.)

Format refers to the proportions, size, or orientation of a composition or live area.

Grids are structural systems for organizing content in graphic design projects. They include both horizontal and vertical thresholds or guidelines indicating where text and images should be placed.

Ground (or *background*) is like negative space. It is an area of space without elements or form.

Guides (also called guidelines) are repositionable horizontal and vertical markers used for measuring and alignment purposes. Guides are visible on screen but do not print unless the user specifically chooses to do so.

Gutter is the space between two columns of text and/or between two pages in a book. The space between two pages is also called the fold or the spine.

Hierarchy is the relative importance of elements within a composition.

Hue is another term for *color*. The two words are used interchangeably.

Hyphenation is the marked syllabic division of words.

Ideation is the process of generating ideas and expressing them either through diagrams or visual explorations.

Inspiration is the process of being visually or mentally stimulated. Many design concepts begin with inspiration.

Kerning is the space between two characters of text. To achieve even spacing between letters, kerning is often needed.

Live area is the space in which a design exists. The term is primarily used when referring to screen-based design such as websites, app designs, or motion graphics.

Manipulation in design is the change or alteration of a visual from its original form. Changing color or distorting line quality are both examples of digital manipulation.

Margins refer specifically to the space between the edge of the page and a marker or threshold where content begins. They can be set and repositioned in most design software programs.

Mode is the way an artwork or design was generated. The same subject can be represented using different modes such as photography, drawing, or collage. In graphics software, the "mode" of a file changes what type of color system is used to render it.

Modular refers to a grid system with both horizontal and vertical divisions of space. Each module indicates alignment points where content can be placed.

Monotones (or *monochromatic*) are color schemes produced using a single color plus its tints and shades.

Mounting refers to a process where one substrate is fixed to another. In graphic design projects, paper printouts or drawings are usually pasted onto board or Foamcore before being presented.

Narrative is the story. In design, narrative can be both textual and visual. For example, imagery and other visuals can be used to complement or refer to particular aspects of the text, or simple shapes may be used on their own to create a visual narrative.

Neutrals are colors including black, white, gray, and muted tones of brown or beige.

Negative space is the space around visual elements.

Orphan refers to instances where a word exists by itself on a line. Orphans should be avoided. To do so, use tracking or hyphenation to bring the word up onto the line before or to bring another word down onto the line with it.

Permissions or photo release is a legal release or waiver signed by a model (for photography) or by the originator or owner of an artwork granting another person the permission to publish or reproduce the photograph or artwork.

Pixilation refers to digital or digitized imagery that has been enlarged or distorted so the image breaks up and individual pixels can be seen. Pixilation of imagery should generally be avoided.

Production can be either digital or physical and may involve printing or coding, depending on what type of design is being made.

Proofing is the testing of a print or a design before a piece goes to final production. For example, one will proof or test colors several times before printing a large banner or long book.

Representational images are images that are clearly recognizable and refer to life. For example, a representational image of a dog will look similar to how the dog appears in life.

Research is the systematic gathering and investigation of facts, ideas, or visuals related to a particular subject or a project.

Rule is another word for lines and is specifically used when describing lines in design compositions.

Sans serif typefaces do not have extra elements added to the strokes of the letterforms.

Saturation (also called **chroma**) is the intensity, strength, or purity of a color without the addition of black or white.

Scale is the relative size of an item in a design composition. The term can be used as a verb as in "to scale" an image.

Serifs are small elements added to the main strokes of letterforms. Typefaces are classified by whether they have these elements or not.

Shade is the variation of a color plus black.

Spreads are two pages of a book or another design deliverable.

Static is lacking in movement or action. In design, a space or element that is static is considered less interesting and generally undesirable.

Strategy is a plan of action designed to achieve specific goals and objectives.

Style is the appearance or distinctive visual character. An image may be drawn in either an *abstract* or *representational* style, for example.

Subtractive color is a model based on the primary colors red, blue, and yellow; it mimics the spectrum of colors used by artists.

Temperature is the perceived warmth or coolness of a color.

Thresholds (also called *flow lines*) are points or lines used by designers to align or place elements in a layout. Guides are often used to indicate thresholds.

Tint is the variations of a color plus white.

Tracking is the space between the characters of text or words.

Trimming flush is trimming to the edge of the composition. If something is trimmed flush it has no border.

Type family refers to the collection of different weights and iterations of a typeface.

Type foundries own the rights to the design of typefaces and will sell digital versions of a typeface to the general public. The cost of a typeface varies considerably based on who designed it and whether it comes with an extended family or not.

Typesetting is the visual arrangement of text. The term dates back to when individual letters of metal type were "set" together to form the compositional arrangements used in printing. Today, typesetting is primarily digital and refers to working with (or "setting") large amounts of text.

Typographer is someone who designs typefaces. They may be commissioned to design a typeface for a particular client, or they may initiate the design of a new typeface on their own.

Value is the relative lightness or darkness of a color. (See Chapter 4.)

Warm colors are hues with underlying tones of red.

Weight is the thickness or thinness of a typeface.

Widow is a single line of text in a column by itself. Widows should be avoided because they cause unnecessary breaks in the text.

INDEX

&Larry (Singapore), 48, 66, 69, 80, 107, 118, 147, 155, 165, 188
3M Australia, Corporate Headquarters, 101

A

Abstract images, 151, 155, 232
Abstraction, 151, 153–157, 232
Accordion fold, 222
Acme (Paris, France), 17, 56, 70, 76, 97, 145, 152, 220
Activating, 55, 72, 232
Active, 55, 66, 232
Active words, exercise, 140
Additive color, 85, 232
Adhesion. *See* Glues and adhesion
Adhesive binding, 218
Adobe Capture, 105
Adobe.com, 19, 105, 131
Adobe Illustrator, 18, 68, 103, 152, 167, 168, 172, 175, 195
Adobe InDesign, 18, 195, 214
Adobe Kuler, 105
Adobe Photoshop, 18, 68, 103, 109, 167, 172, 174, 175
Advertising design, 9, 12
Afterhours (Kent, UK), 79, 81
AI (Adobe Illustrator Artwork file), 168
AIGA Toledo, 44
Albers, Joseph, 102
Aligning, elements, 76
Alignment
   centered text, 129
   flush left, 128
   flush right text, 129
   justified text, 129
   spacing and, 128–136
Anagrama (Nuevo Leon, Mexico), 64, 77, 80, 98, 104, 119, 122, 163, 210, 212
Analog, 151, 232
Analogous harmonies, color wheel, 93
Anthropomorphism, 41
Application design, 13
Arrangement. *See* Layout
Art, graphic design, 10
Artiana Wynder (New York), 92
Artists' primary colors, 88
Art-making techniques, images, 161, 162
Ascenders, 117, 132, 142
Assets, 9, 20, 27, 232
Asymmetry, 73, 198
Audience, 9, 10, 27, 34, 42–43
Aufuldish & Warinner (San Anselmo, California), 42, 108, 124, 137, 176, 194

B

B12 (Scottsdale, Arizona), 13, 134, 156, 174, 200
Backing up, 209, 226, 228
Balance, 72
Barrel fold, 223
Baseline, 117
Basic color wheel, 90
Baskerville, John, 143
Bequeth Liz DeLuna (New York), 30–31
Berlow, David, 144
Bezier curves, 68, 167
Bianca Alcantara (New York), 148, 171
Binding, 209
   common punching patterns, 220
   loop, 220
   metal spiral, 220
   perfect, 218
   presentation, 218–220
   saddle stitch, 219
   sewn, 221
   spiral, 220
Black, 107, 115, 232
Bleed/bleeding, 55, 76, 232
Blindness, color, 98
Bodoni, Giambattista, 143
Body copy, 115, 232
Body text, 115, 125, 141, 232
Book covers, 52
Book weight, 115, 119
Border, mounting with, 225
Brainstorming, 27, 232
   exercise, 52
   framing the design problem, 37
   free association, 36–37
   ideas with actions, 39
   using connections, 38
Brief, 27, 28
Bright colors, 98
Brightness, 85, 89, 232
Bruketa&Zinic (Zagreb, Croatia), 39, 43, 49, 110, 126, 132, 139, 160, 162, 221

C

California Collage of the Arts, 42
Cap height, 117
Career outlook, 22, 24
Carter, Matthew, 143, 144
Cassio Saboia (New York), 144
Cast Iron Design (Boulder, Colorado), 14, 32, 51, 69, 72, 81, 169, 213
Cheah Wei Chun, CLANHOUSE (Singapore), 58, 75, 87, 147, 170, 174, 175, 180, 184, 186, 200, 202

Christmas Gifts (Studio Rašić), 227
Chroma, 85, 234
Cliché, 27, 35
Client, 9, 20
Clustering, elements, 76
CMYK (cyan, magenta, yellow and black), 88, 107, 113, 212, 214
Collage, 165, 166
Color, 85, 232
   blindness, 98
   bright, 98
   compositions based on Itten's contrasts, 103
   contrast and, 111
   cool, 96
   custom, 108
   dark, 97
   description of, 86–87
   design software for working with, 105
   emphasizing with, 186, 187
   hierarchy and, 110
   light, 97
   neutral, 95
   printing black, 107
   repetition, 110
   selection, 106
   step-by-step guide to working with, 105
   subjective associative meaning, 87
   systems of primary, 88
   type and, 141
   value, 95
   visible spectrum, 87
   warm, 96
Color-aid paper production, 103
Color palette, 85, 232
   choosing a, 104–111
   color and hierarchy, 110
   color in use, 111
   color repetition, 110
   color selection, 106
   contrast and color, 111
   custom colors, 108
   design software, 105
   dominant/subordinate system, 106
   image-based, 109
   one-color, 107
   printing black, 107
   step-by-step guide, 105
   two-color, 108
Color Scheme Designer (Paletton's), 105
Color theory, 85, 99–100, 102, 232
Color wheels
   analogous harmonies, 93

complementary hues, 92
   diagrams, 90–94
   Itten's, 102
   monochromatic hue, 94
   primary hues, 90
   secondary hues, 91
   split complements, 92
   terminology and, 88–98
   tertiary hues, 91
   tetrad harmonies, 94
   triad harmonies, 93
Column grids, 201–202
Columns, 179, 232
Commercial artist, 9, 14
Communication design, 9, 10
Communication designers, 11, 13
Comp, 209, 210, 232
Complementary colors, 85
Complementary hues, color wheel, 92
Composition, 55, 59, 82, 232
Compositional space, 59, 232
Concept, 9, 16, 27, 33, 35, 55, 60, 232
Condensed, 115, 119
Connotation, 151, 157
Construction, color, 102
Constructional grids, 200
Content, 60
Content sharing, 17
Context, 27, 60
Contract work, 9, 25
Contrast, 55, 70, 79, 232
   color and, 111
   color compositions, 103
   emphasis, 80
   figure-ground, 70
Cool colors, 85, 96, 232
Copyright, 151, 176, 232
Cords, Annette, 103
Craft, 9, 47, 224
Creasing, 209
Creating images, 160–165
Creative/upper-level design, job categories and titles, 24
Critique, 27
   analysis and, 49–50
   discussion points for, 51
   tips for giving feedback, 51
Cropping, 66, 67, 121, 174, 232
Custom colors, 108
Custom photography, 170
Custom visuals, 13

D

Daniela Carusone (New York), 120
Daniella Circelli (Bronx, New York), 164

PICTURE CREDITS

All reasonable attempts have been made to trace, clear, and credit the copyright holders of the images reproduced in this book. However, if any credits have been inadvertently omitted, the publisher will endeavor to incorporate amendments in future editions.

Acmé Paris pp. 17c, 56, 70l, 76r, 97c, 145l&bl, 152/ **Afterhours** p. 79br/ **Anagrama** pp. 64b, 77, 80tr, 98t, 104l, 119t, 122, 163tr, 210tl, 212r/ **&Larry** pp. 48, 66bl, 69t, 80t, 107t, 118t, 147t, 155tl, 165r, 188cl/ **Artiana Wynder** p. 92l/ **Atelier Bundi AG** pp. 33t, 35br, 38b, 67r, 95r, 139tr, 171bl, 176r/ **Courtesy of and ©Aufuldish & Warriner** pp. 42, 108, 124b, 137b, 176l, 194tl&tr/ **B12** pp. 13b, 134tl, 156bl&tr, 174t, 190tr, 200t/ **Bianca Alcantara** p. 148b, 171r/ **Bruketa&Zinic OM** pp. 39b, 43, 49, 110r, 126, 132tl&bl, 139b, 157b, 160tl&bl, 162, 221bl/ **Cassio Saboia** p. 144/ **Cast Iron Design** pp. 14b, 32, 51, 69c&b, 72t, 81t, 169t, 213/ **Cheah Wei Chun/Clanhouseonline.com** pp. 58r, 75b, 87t&c, 147b, 170br, 174b, 175b, 180, 184tr, 186t, 200br, 202t&c/ **Dan Lemperle** p. 67tl/ **Daniela Carusone** p. 120br/ **Dedica Group** pp. 19 © 2015 Dedica Group. All rights reserved. 62t Meritage Coffee & Tea LLC. All rights reserved, 173 West Elm© Market. All rights reserved./ **Eduardo Bertone** pp. 13c SEMA Design ©2015, 107b Monsieur Gordo Brewery © 2015. 110l&c Pacharan Zoco ©2015. 163l Bear Flag Wines ©2015/ **Elaine Lustig Cohen** p. 161c/ **Elephant Design** p. 47br/ **Esen Karol Design Ltd.** pp. 25t, 141t, 188cr, 193tr&br, 206, 216/ **Fabricio Augusto Lima dos Santos** p. 36/ **©Felipe Taborda** pp. 25b, 63r, 71bl, 79bl/ **Garth Walker** pp.18, 73t&br/ **Genevieve Hitchings** p. 87b/ **©Gerwin Schmidt** 2017 pp. 58l, 129r, 145tr, 160fr, 164l, 183tr, 184c, 190tl, 191l&bl, 197t,cr(2)/ **ggrafik** pp. 65l, 86, 95bl, 127t, 184b, 189b, 200bl, 212t/ **Hatch Design** p. 34 Client: Krave Jerky, Agency: Hatch Design, Creative Directors: Joel Templin, Katie Jain, Designers: Will Ecke, Anna Hurley (Whole Foods/Artisanal Illustrations), Photographer: Sarah Remington, Copywriter: Lisa Pemrick/ **Idalea Cinquiemani** pp. 169b, 211b/ **Izyum Creative Group** pp. 16, 17b, 37/ **Jenn Stucker** pp. 44–45/ **Jessica Monteavaro Garbin** pp. 36, 46, 90r, 93bl, 167, 204–205/ **Katherine Mias** pp. 15b, 47bl, 159, 165l/ **© Kuhlmann Leavitt Inc.** pp. 13t, 59r, 75t, 88r, 125t, 128l, 132r/ **Liz DeLuna** pp. 30–31, 121, 121bl Bailey

Kass courtesy of Liz DeLuna, 140, 166 / **Liz Marcotte** p. 93br/ © **Lotta Nieminen** pp. 22t, 72b, 155bl, 161b, 196/ **Maria Torres** p. 91l/ **Metalli Lindberg** pp. 96bl, 104r, 170c/ **Michael LaGattuta** p. 142tl/ **Parabureau,** Designer: Andrija Mudnic, Creative Director: Igor Stanisljevic pp. 88l, 89b, 97b, 117t, 123r, 127b, 194br, 201t/ **©Pérezramerstorfer Studio** pp. 40, 41b, 57, 61t/ **Project Projects** pp. 29t, 61b, 78t, 107c, 111, 134br, 136, 187t&l, 203/ **Rašić+Vrabec** pp. 11, 33b, 63t, 71tfl, 97tr, 116r, 146, 153tl, 156br, 164r, 175t, 198cl&cl, 227/ **Rebecca Brooker** p. 142b/ **©Rebecca Foster Design** 2015 pp. 71tc&r, 76t&c, 79t, 82, 128r, 188br, 192tr,cr,br/ **©Sägenvier** pp. 35bl, 38t, 39t, 41t, 95tl/ **©Seitaro Design, Inc.** pp. 154, 157t, 158bl/ **Skolos-Wedell** pp. 161tr, 170t/ **©Sonsoles** pp. 68t, 211t, 218b/ **Steven Verdile** p. 92r/ **James Kirkup and Studio Beuro** pp. 59l, 89b, 96r, 98b, 99, 129l/ **Created/Designed by Taylor Slyder** pp. 91b, 94bl/ **THERE Design** pp. 15t, 17t, 22b, 73bl, 89c, 101, 137c, 158tr, 182t&b, 187b, 188t, 195cr&br, 197b, 199tl&r, 219/ **This Is Folly** p. 10 Client: This Is Folly, Art Direction/ Design: Holly Robbins & John Moes. 14t Client: ecoThynk, Art Direction/Design: John Moes. 29b Client: Organic Design Operatives (ODO), Art Direction/Design: John Moes & Holly Robbins. 50b Client: Currents Apartment Homes, Art Direction/Design: John Moes & Holly Robbins. 106 Client: Organic Design Operatives (ODO), Art Direction/ Design: John Moes & Holly Robbins, Photography: Todd Hafermann Photography. 109b, 195tl&cr, 210br, Client: Reneu Concepts/Ikaati, Photography: Kendall Photographs. 214–215 Client: MiX, Art Direction/ Design: John Moes & Holly Robbins./ **Verônica de Araujo Farias** p. 94br/ **Victor Bregante** pp. 60, 120bl.

©2017 Apple Inc., All rights reserved. p. 156 tl/ **Creative commons:** p. 139 Mark Buckawicki /**Getty Images:** p. 23 ullstein bild/Contributor p. 62bc morabird; p. 62br Raquel Maria Carbonelli Pagola/Contributor; p. 74 Jeroen Fortgens; p. 120 michellealbert; p. 172 Photos by R A Kearton; p. 190 Paper Boat Creative (woman with pink hair), Carmen Gold/Eye Em (hand holding photo), Alessandro Michelazzi/ Eye Em (woman w/camera and hat); p. 191 Angie Ravelo Photography; p. 199 SpiffyJ.

ACKNOWLEDGMENTS

I would like to thank Lee Ripley and the rest of the team at Bloomsbury for their ongoing support and efforts to see *Introduction to Graphic Design* through from proposal to publication. I am also grateful to the design studios and individuals who were willing to share examples of their work and of their process. These visual examples help bring the text to life. Brenno Pinto, Daniella Circelli and Mike LaGattuta produced the diagrams highlighting different principles of design. Their contribution has been invaluable and I am grateful for their patience and attention to detail as we worked to identify the best visual representations of various aspects of the design process.

Finally, this book is dedicated to my students at St. John's University. They provide endless inspiration and never fail to keep me humble.